Potency

Marie-Louise von Franz, Honorary Patron

**Studies in Jungian Psychology
by Jungian Analysts**

Daryl Sharp, General Editor

POTENCY

Masculine Aggression as a Path to the Soul

Eugene Monick

Also by Eugene Monick in this series:

Phallos: Sacred Image of the Masculine (1987)

Castration and Male Rage: The Phallic Wound (1991)

Library and Archives Canada Cataloguing in Publication

Monick, Eugene, 1929-
Potency: Masculine Aggression as a path to the Soul / Eugene Monick.

(Studies in Jungian psychology by Jungian analysts; 114)

Includes bibliographical references and index.

ISBN 1-894574-15-X

1. Aggressiveness. 2. Masculinity.
3. Men—Psychology.
4. Jungian psychology.
I. Title. II. Series

BF692.5.M66 2006   155.6'32   C2005-906925-2

INNER CITY BOOKS
Box 1271, Station Q, Toronto, ON M4T 2P4, Canada.

Telephone (416) 927-0355 / Fax (416) 924-1814

Web site: www.innercitybooks.net / E-mail: admin@innercitybooks.net

Honorary Patron: Marie-Louise von Franz.
Publisher and General Editor: Daryl Sharp.
Senior Editor: Victoria B. Cowan.

INNER CITY BOOKS was founded in 1980 to promote the
understanding and practical application of the work of C.G. Jung.

Cover: *La Grande Boucle* (The Big Loop, detail), sculpture by Bernard Métais
    near Pau, France, on the road to prehistoric caves in the Basque Pyrenées,
    honoring the Tour de France. See also page 145. Photos by Eugene Monick.

Printed and bound in Canada by University of Toronto Press Incorporated

Contents

See final pages for descriptions of other Inner City Books

Introduction

There are two things that the reader should note at the outset. One is that I use potency here as a masculine word. It comes to us from the old Latin *potens* meaning to be able, to have power. The reference in this work is to phallos as male erection, that which delivers seed and stimulates females and therefore is the male instrument of generation, what was known to the Greeks as the signifier of the masculine.[1] Phallos is the signifier of masculinity because its fate is to be the means of penetration and insemination, thus moving human genes into the next generation. In order to do this, a man's penis must transform from easy soft, so as to be a means of urination, to erect, hard—able to penetrate the female body and plunge again and again toward its goal. That is powerful action, giving meaning to potency. Penetration and subsequent ejaculation are the root source of masculine symbolism. Based in the male body—on its behavior and fate— potency has become the psychological as well as physical talismanic image of identity for maleness.

The second notable item is that phallos makes the succession of life possible from the perspective of masculine participation. But phallos also provides a sublime experience of intimate pleasure and affirmation that feeds a man's knowledge of himself and his personal pride. Why the evolution of male development combined genetic continuity with the sublime experience of pleasure and affirmation is an intriguing question. It is touched upon here in my chapter on ecstasy, but otherwise it is beyond the scope of this current work.

My writing here centers upon male potency, that which makes possible the sublime experience of intimate personal pleasure and affirmation. Mine is a mystical quest more than an

---

1 I use the Greek spelling rather than the Roman *phallus* since the Greek is closer to the province of symbol.

7

intellectual one. Intellect must be used but, as I see it, intellect is handmaiden to mystery, requiring something of a poetic, even lyrical tone, which is the mode of my writing. The source of mystery is, at first, sensation, for a man experiences the exquisite tenderness of his erection each time it comes upon him. He wants to re-experience what is dear to him, over and over again. But a deeper understanding of the experience of phallos for men requires intuition even more than reason, for intuition emerges from the unconscious and connects a man's self-awareness with the depths. Mystery emerges in an almost alchemical way. (I have often had the subjective sense that I am a medieval monk doing an illuminated manuscript at my computer, exposing a secret open to everyone but valued only by the initiated.)

Oh, the writing must pay some attention to being straightforward and twenty-first century (after all, it is about phallos and phallos has been commandeered by patriarchy), but there is a limit beyond which "head' expression cannot go, without losing connection with soul. A great thing about phallos is that every man has been, in some important way, initiated, the root meaning of mystery. Some readers will find this right-brain propensity of mine exasperating. I too find it that, certainly, for it complicates my writing. But it serves as a door into the unconscious.

Some presuppositions

Each gender has power and primacy, as do the bodies of each gender. Potency, as I use the word here, is my way of speaking of the intensity of power grounded in male instinct, emanating from deeply within the hidden conjunction of psyche and body. Potency is seen in erection, the energy of the male groin, leading to male penetration as a force behind ongoing life. An erection may be more or less subjectively powerful according to the mood of its perceiver but it is never, psychologically/emotionally, without power. That power is universal, or in Jung's terms, archetypal. It varies in cultures as in individuals. But it is always present as definition, mystery, prompt and metaphor. It moves a male beyond himself, into and around his opposite, bespeaking a man's subjective identity, his place and his function. Phallos evinces new life in reproduction, but also in excitement, the expression of male intensity and in the implication of a man's purpose and his promise.

The English language does not ordinarily give gender to nouns, but since I use potency as erection in this work, potency inevitably has gender. Of course, females have *yang* or phallic psychological qualities, and in physical qualities as well, although usually in shorter supply since phallos is clearly a masculine attribute, fed by testosterone of which hormone the female has far less. Phallos and testes organically function to express male participation in life as present satisfaction and future consequence. Masculine characteristics always refer, or are attributed to, phallos as essential masculine signifier. An energized penis, full of blood and heavily intent upon the pleasure of penetration leading to ejaculation is an analogical god appearing from primal and inaccessible source in physical form—e.g., Michelangelo's Sistine divinity touching man with his phallic finger—as a picture of that which gives male erection its spiritual and psychological importance.

C.G. Jung paid little attention to the psychology of masculinity since males were always in charge in Victorian Switzerland and Jung, in that sense, was a man of his time. Women were dependent upon men, the leaders. Psychoanalytic fundament, inherited from Freud, rested easily upon the presumption of male dominance—patriarchy. No one had to define or explain masculinity any more than one had to define or explain mountains.

As I write today, aware of an ever-enlarging international feminism as well as of democracy, and the enormous struggle for individual freedom everywhere, one can no longer take inherent male supremacy for granted. The collapse, or impending collapse, of patriarchy—that is, the social dominance of males as an assumed cultural given—is on our doorstep if not already in the house. Men feel this change deeply. Almost everywhere, be-

ing born male has made a man feel entitled, so deeply has patriarchy been the common parlance of ego culture.

Becoming unentitled can make men insecure, angry and
pathologically violent, as though they face the threat of castration, as though their metaphorical birthright were suddenly sto-
len, leaving them vulnerable in their self-regard. For how can
men function without their traditional ability to design and control their environment?

I intend my work to address that question.

This book is based upon my Jungian and, in some ways, Christian suppositions, for those, along with my liberal political
leanings, are the main ideological factors in my life. It is more of
a Jungian book than a Christian book and more of a Christian
book than a liberal book. The reader has a right to know this.

For the reader unfamiliar with Jung or Christianity, bookstores
and libraries are full of resources. Read Jung himself. Start with
Volume 7 of the Collected Works, *Two Essays on Analytical
Psychology,* or Jung's autobiography *Memories, Dreams, Reflections.* If one were to read Christianity in a Monickian direction—one that is traditionally Anglican and thus in the middle
between ancient and modern, liturgical and prophetic, Catholic
and Protestant, one might be well advised to avoid explicitly
right-wing and/or fundamentalist commentaries.

For the purposes of this introduction, I can but mention
briefly one issue that draws upon both Jung and Christianity.

Jung, as I understand him, believed that nothing "exterior" to
one's personal psyche—and one's personal psyche as embedded
in the collective unconscious—should dominate a conscious person's life. To understand that statement requires knowledge that
"one's personal psyche," my phrase, has a transpersonal dimension, an ability to reach or sense a reality that is beyond what
Freud, and Jung after him, called the ego, the "I" quality of personal experience. The question of what is exterior, for the purposes of this note, has to do with ego and ego's evaluations and
ego's essential connection to and expression of the exterior

world. Without an "I" one can hardly begin. The idea here is
that one's ego is the means, the organ, as it were, by which one
moves out from personal experience in order to perceive that
which goes on beyond one's borders. That is the world. How one
evaluates one's perceptions is an important further matter but
not specifically my object in this writing, aside from my take on
patriarchy.

Not so the soul. Soul belongs to a transcendental order that
passes beyond the ego into a sense of depth. Soul represents that
aspect of experience that is not as limited as ego since soul is not
constricted by rational or conscious boundaries. Soul sinks deeper
into the psyche. Soul is the translation of the Greek word *psyche*. Soul is more closely related to subjective experience as ego
is more closely related to objective experience, viz.: how one
feels and thinks about life, liberty and the pursuit of happiness.
Christian scripture reflects the matter this way: "Has not God
made foolish the wisdom of the world?" (I Cor. 1:20)[2] Soul here
speaks through the letter of Paul, having the capacity, due to its
transcendent nature, to know that "the wisdom of the world"
cannot be depended upon if taken at its face value, that something other than "the world" is necessary and of greater value,
and that soul is the organ of that discernment. Soul is the way of
knowing that a painting moves one, that a landscape has a quality of the ultimate, that a certain person is one's beloved. Soul,
then, has a subversive effect upon ego. It can influence the ego
to doubt itself. But only if one moves beyond ego and listens to
the comforts and discomforts of soul.

For Jung, one's reaction to symbol is an expression of soul's
impact upon ego. Symbol stands for that which rational ego cannot manufacture or understand since ego, by itself, does not go
deeply enough into the collective unconscious. Along with concrete ego reality in modest amounts, particularly ego's capacity
to discern importance, symbol is arbiter of psychic truth. Symbol

---

2 **Revised Standard Veersion of the Holy Bible, used throughout.**

tends toward abstraction in situations where literalism cannot express depth. One person can stare at symbol and never see more than is there in lines and colors and space. Another can see in what one is watching a kind of revelation. The collective unconscious, specifically the realm of the archetypes, lying as it does beneath the personal unconscious, moves far beyond Freud's concept of the unconscious as the repository of repressed and forgotten personal experience. Jung's collective unconscious has a teleological function, bringing his thought close to the spiritual world acknowledged by religion, though religion it be not. It is soul. On a personal level, the way to find the second, internal world is through dreams, fantasy, imagination, feelings and affection—what happens in the privacy of personal awareness, where a man encounters anima, soul and his own closeness to the feminine, and hence to completeness.

What is interior, neglected, even denigrated, since the Enlightenment, is the domain of subjective experience, the domain of psyche, the domain of soul—Jung's primary interest. The disjuncture between what one "should" believe (and the issue is cultural and political as well as religious authority) and what one finds happening in one's own private thoughts, hopes and life is what pushes people toward Jung. Patriarchy is the common religion of our time, accepted as masculine essence, rather than phallos. Especially men rarely seriously question it. There would seem to be no alternative.

A radical aspect of Jung was his taking of his own personal psychic experience with an elemental seriousness, unusual even for one with his astonishingly introverted propensity, expanded by his prodigious scholarship. Jung searched out antecedents for his own and his patients' experience in material from the unconscious and in cultural history. Since "the world," to use Biblical language—that is, the "exterior"—is what we can know both rationally and sensorily, Jung, in his extraordinary curiosity and openness to, say, the occult, came to be seen as otherworldly, unempirical, an oddity in a post-Enlightenment rational world.

He held that modern culture had lost its fundamental bearings. The pressure of rational conformity against the background of an invisible collective unconscious, a buried prehistorical evolutionary past, was for Jung a primary cause of humanity's inner distress. To remedy this situation, he thought one should pay attention to dreams and other surges from the depths, to human history and the images that emerge from contemplation and reflection. All of them indicate where the points of inner conflict might be. Such a process would be impossible were there no soul. Reason, essential as it is, is no final solution since reason, *per se,* permits no mystery.

Jung felt that the pseudo-liberated ego was a secret and insidious plague hidden beneath an illusion of progress. Ego played all of its tricks, well established by Freud, to justify its domination but ego itself has a nefarious side. It separates and isolates us from our psychic foundation in soul. Here one can see a paradoxical religious impulse at work in Jung. He rejected his doctrinal Christian origin. What he did not reject was the reality of an unseen world.

Jung's way was to return to a possibility of original wholeness (the Biblical implications of this are not difficult to decipher) without surrendering the accomplishments of modern life. This could happen through the union—or even more, for a modern person, the re-union—of the collective unconscious with the world of ego-consciousness, the two opposites Jung took pains to explicate and rejoin. That process Jung called transformation.

Jung was a skeptic. He was a Swiss Reformed Christian by family background but he could not believe specific doctrines expounded by his clergy father, however much he was influenced by their moral and ethical implications. He was, as I have come to be, an extra-Christian, one no longer beholden to doctrine as defined by religious authority or scriptural literalism, yet profoundly influenced by its world view. Jung did not abandon belief, however much he may have claimed that he no longer believed in God but he knew.[3] It was redirected. The criteria shifted. The authority became inner experience.

That made Jung into what even many Jungians (in our day of rational dominance) once denied—a mystic. It was within himself that he found a new way to authority.

The collective unconscious could not be made to behave according to the dictates of reason and the desires of ego. What pressed up from the depths was *daimon,* or *numen,* experienced as an inner, living voice. Numen emerged as a divinely felt influence, a spirit, as though it had a mind of its own. This Jung called *instinct,* manifesting in human consciousness via the collective unconscious through human culture, in art, in religion, in daily experience and imagination.

What was mystical for Jung was the soul, the organ, so to speak, of the "other world," unseen, immeasurable, full of contradictions, a mixture of beauty and horror. Soul is the core of the "inside," that which is radically subjective, having an authority of its own and available only to the subject; it is what happens to a man at the moment he knows he is in love. Jung believed that soul is one's relationship with psyche.

Anyone who *knows* something personal that no one else can know in quite the same way has within a touch of the mystic. The problem for many is that we believe, in an obedient way, that only when something is generally accepted is it true. Why else did I drive my streets during the Bush/Kerry presidential campaign looking for Kerry signs on front lawns? The moment that I saw one, the need I had for affirmation was satisfied. Almost simultaneously, I suspected that my seeing it objectively proved nothing, as the election results demonstrated. Yet my wandering eye told me about my soul.

Something else needs to be said. I understand that which is mystical to be an intensely personal experience, something that

---

3 "The 'Face to Face' Interview," in William McGuire and R.F.C. Hull, eds. *C.G. Jung Speaking: Interviews and Encounters,* p. 426.

cannot be described in purely rational terms. That makes writing a book in a mystical direction difficult, since writing is primarily a rational/intellectual exercise. Mystical experiences are just that, experiences. I write here not in a didactic mode, a "head" mode, as it were, as is the masculine logos way, but in an expressionistic, almost free-associated way, allowing the idea I seek to unravel to do so along a somewhat idiosyncratic path, which is, strangely, for a book on masculinity, a much more feminine mode. I take courage to so include the feminine as a mystical element in masculine psyche from a remarkable essay by an Israeli Jungian analyst on the Kabbalah and its relationship to alchemy; it plumbs the flow of energy in an alchemical painting as illustrating "the flow between the upper and lower vessels [that is, the soul and the ego] and the vessel in the painting [as it always is symbolically] is female . . . this is how feeling works . . . clarifying why this flow moves within a female system of symbols. . . . The presence of God in the world is a female principle; this is the symbolic essence of the *Shekhinah.* Whereas the male does and creates (doing), the female is present [I would say within the male], senses and feels (being)."4

So I must ask the reader to look within and, as an analysand said to me recently, move into something of a feminine tone of being, take a risk that the tone is part of the story, quite apart from patriarchal dogma, without too much worry that being generous and liberal indicates an insecure masculinity. The present American patriarchal schema would have us take anything but belligerence as less than manly. Time tells us that we men need to define masculinity quite apart from patriarchy, for patriarchy diminishes sensitivity, the secret mystic otherworld of life and the genuine beauty of maleness.

So take something of a trip with me; bring along your private and synchronistic associations that fit into the flow of the theme being presented. Structural purity is not my manner of

4 See Micha Ankori, "A Mytho-Psychological Study of the Biblical Legacy," p. 15.

discourse. Phallos is certainly structural and fits into Jung's notion that logos is the masculine standard. But one must at times jump over established ego boundaries, since individuation, Jung's term for psychological maturity, is never wholly stereotypical.

Infused in phallos, and the cause of its erection, is blood. And here is paradox, another important Jungian notion. Blood probably should be seen as archetypally feminine, so connected is it with menses and childbirth. Yet beneath blood in body, and its excited presence in erection, is that which makes a man's blood "boil," a psychic enticement by its opposite, its mystery—the source of excitement. Enchantment might be the word for what happens to a man, for the notion of enchantment calls forth a presence of the sorcery of love. The moment one considers enchantment one can know how a man might leave the realm of logos/word/mind in his brush against logos's opposite, eros, the feminine. In so doing, he discovers himself anew. He becomes somewhat spellbound, his mind becomes woozy since he cannot think well; he is out of his element, embarked on a tour of duty to a foreign land, the promise of a beloved, the origin-love that is not forbidden. For this to happen, a man must find himself strangely opened to his own hidden, repressed, contrasexual aspects, what Jung calls his anima—buried, antagonistic feminine qualities, remnants of what Freud called his bisexuality, aspects which portend to open a dimension of existence which he had no idea even existed in him, to say nothing of dominating his consciousness. That is an internal process called projection. Its positive face is also called falling in love.

Shadow

It will not have escaped the notice of some readers that I applaud and celebrate masculine aggression without so far spelling out an essential caveat, namely the negative or shadow (in Jungspeak) factor that exists in all psychological reality and particularly, in this essay, in penetration. In phallic aggression, many think that the shadow is more than a factor; that it is the whole of the thing. Many women at the 1995 Friends' Conference, where my investigation continued, thought so, about which more later. Their experience with men might have encouraged such an evaluation and if so, they have experienced something of the ambivalence of a powerful archetype, an aspect of psychic reality which every mature person needs to know and prepare for. But their experience, if such it was, important as it is, is not the whole story, even as my take on phallic aggression is not the whole story. My positive take on phallos needs balance. So does theirs. My paean of praise for male aggression is, I think, a form of acknowledging reality but it needs my admission of what Jung calls shadow if it is to come anywhere close to what human beings know in daily life.

A paramount and radical part of Jung's psychology is his notion that all of psyche is ambivalent, top to bottom. Good is always mixed with evil, evil with good, even as making a nourishing soup requires the death of once-living animal and vegetable components. One heats the contents even if one consumes the soup cold. Nothing is so bad that something good cannot be found within it; nothing so good that evil does not lurk at its boundaries. Jung's treatment of Job,[5] problematic as it may be, was an extraordinary explication of his conviction that life, even the life of God, has a built-in "on the fence" quality about it.[6] There are many who think that "Answer to Job" is the most original piece that Jung ever wrote. Jung called the negative side of something good its shadow, even as a material reality (one's body, say), relative to the sun, casts a shadow.

Since penetration is the *Ding an sich* of phallos—it must be hard and stiff in order to penetrate—then negative penetration, probably most nefariously manifesting in rape, cannot be ig-

---

5 See "Answer to Job," *Psychology and Religion: East and West.* CW 11, pars. 553ff. [CW refers throughout to *The Collected Works of C.G. Jung.*]

6 See Monick, *Evil, Sexuality and Disease in Grünewald's Body of Christ,* Spring Publications, 1993.

nored.[7] Rape is violation, but rape no more invalidates masculine aggression than does sour milk invalidate the breast. That said, it is incumbent upon me to acknowledge the shadow aspects of phallic aggression and to seriously regret them, as I do, even while concentrating on the positive side of phallic aggression, as has been my intention. I do not regret focusing on the necessity of male aggression, for otherwise phallos would have no point. I do not feel a need to give examples of male violence toward women and children and, indeed, other men. The front pages of the daily news are full of all that, the current Iraq war being a prime example. What is necessary for men is to turn away from physical, psychological and political battery—patriarchal domination—not natural organ and symbolic disposition, to break ground for building a new world without surrendering our prized and urgently important possession, a source of our *gnosis*.

Men have taken their fair share of hard knocks in recent years, much due to our careless, dominating, ignorant and ego-absorbed behavior together with the ghoulish triumphalism of patriarchy. Men who don't like this must do more than complain about it, such action itself being a sign of transformation. We must all work to accomplish democracy, and to relish and celebrate equality among human beings.

Male violence raises the question of why men sometimes have the need to dominate. Violence is destructive toward both the person and the society that patriarchal men claim to protect. Christian people can be naïve about God. A woman who feels ravished by a man she does not enjoy may be unaware of the causes of her need to give in to his penetration. A man who feels imprisoned by a woman's need may also be unaware of the sources of this feeling in his personal history as much as in her behavior. Such are the issues inherent in male-female, mother-son, father-daughter, father-son, mother-daughter projections. That they occur for a man does not mean that the womb is evil,

---

7 See Bradley A. Te Passke, *Rape and Ritual*, for a psychological study of this subject.

that breast milk is poisonous, that he need feel guilty about his desire to penetrate, as long as he does not feel that the female vessel is made only for his phallos.

Marriage, and patriarchal domination, as a function of societal expectation, can seduce women to give in to domination. Penetration can be that, as shadow phallos, but penetration is also the means of bringing forth new life and contributing to female vitality. Masculine violence toward the female is a sign that the male is out of touch with his own importance to women and his own feminine qualities. It is crucial that a man reflect upon what he does, that he knows that what he has to give to his woman can also be an instrument of destructive aggression.

Violence always is a way to force something that is not happening gracefully. For a man, forcing his erection upon another is the apogee of patriarchy—seen collectively and metaphorically as an extension of domination. Phallos, the means of continuing life, the mystique of union, the seizing of a move toward another world, the realm of spirit implanted upon history, the *modus* of tempest and salute, can be used with terrible manipulation.

The first part of this work, this introduction, is meant to psych out the scene as one Jungian sees it. To psych out anything, one must go within, into the secrets of the heart and soul, as in this book's first chapter. Paying attention, finding what one's soul is saying and feeling is, next to penetration, a man's most masculine activity, a metaphoric expression of potency, intended by psyche to develop a "third ear" for what is going on within him, as Buddhists try to develop a third eye. It is urgent that that ear must be increasingly able to ferret out baloney, to hear falseness, which, after all, is a cheap cut of meat full of fat and not very healthy. Fat kills the heart, as I, who have had a heart attack, know quite well.

The second part of this work is an effort to find four paths that provide alternatives to a man's identifying only with the pattern of patriarchal domination, four alternate ways to celebrate our masculinity. The goal is to attain masculine self-regard and to enjoy ourselves without doing harm to others, and for masculine self-regard to depend upon the strong and indisputable male signification: phallos. We can learn, oppositionally, from President George W. Bush.

The third part of the work is in the heart of the reader. We men must keep looking critically at ourselves, keep reform-ing—phallos gives us a model for that—keep trudging on, knowing that we have soul and heart.

1
Mystical Aspects of Male Sexuality[8]

The most beautiful emotion we can experience is the mystical. It is the
power of all true art and science. He to whom this emotion is a
stranger, who can no longer wonder and stand rapt in awe, is as good
as dead.
—Albert Einstein.

Mysticism is the art of union with Reality.
—Evelyn Underhill.

In persons of mystical genius, the qualities which the stress of normal
life tends to keep below the threshold of consciousness are of enormous strength. In these natural explorers . . . the 'eye of the soul'
is…present in embryo.
—Evelyn Underhill.

I am still a child in mysticism.
—Bede Griffiths, OSB.

What does mysticism really mean? It means the way to attain knowledge. It's close to philosophy, except in philosophy you go horizon-
tally while in mysticism you go vertically.
—Elie Wiesel.

"I think we can say that in and of itself an act of knowledge could
never give access to the truth unless it was prepared, accompanied,
doubled and completed by a certain transformation of the subject; not
of the individual, but of the subject himself in his being as subject."
—Michel Foucault.

---

8 Presented as a lecture, in pre-revised form, to the Philadelphia Seminar of the Inter-Regional Society of Jungian
Analysts, April 1, 2002.

By "mystical genius" in the passage quoted above, Underhill means that a mode of finding a way of life other than ego has been contacted, with genius meaning the natural ability, the spirit of a person, the *numen* which imposes itself from the soul.

Underhill, an Anglican mystic, was not referring to someone specifically saintly. She spent her entire life with ordinary people; insightful though she was, she herself was quite ordinary. What she meant by "genius" in a person was a quality that one experienced and lived in which could be described as inspired, as coming from a *daimon,* an otherworldly characteristic separating the ordinary from the extraordinary, yet quite capable of being both at the same time—exceptional and yet also a part of everyday life. *Daimon* is a spiritlike attribute so strong and characteristic of the person that it would seem to have an otherworldly origin, infused with the tone of an inner guardian that allows one to see and hear a subjective reality that has an intensity quite unlike that of the ego. Underhill calls it "the eye of the soul."

Mystical genius sneaks in between the cracks of ego, surprising ordinary expectation. Wonder hardly ever comes by means of ego. Wonder is always a surprise; it comes by means of something other whispering into one's ear, suggesting, pushing beyond common sense, enticing wonder and belief, not dependent upon proof, whether invited and welcomed or not. It comes as *daimon,* as a visitor from way within, like an infant fresh from the womb. The child did not need the air directly when encased in his mother. Once born, he cannot live without it. So also is the new post-patriarchal man.

In preparation for writing this work I have been aided and encouraged by two books, one fairly new, the other newer. The first is Alain Daniélou's *The Phallus.* The other is *A Mind of Its Own: A Cultural History of the Penis* by David M. Friedman. Little else of consequence has to my knowledge appeared since the publication of my own initial work, *Phal-*

los: Sacred Image of the Masculine, in 1987.[9]

That a man's sexual organ and the symbolic archetypal substratum that stands behind it may have intentionality, that is to say, something of "a mind of its own," coming to a man through his genetic inheritance and the disposition of his body formation, and the wonder these promote, is a lead into the point of this work. Immediately one is led into mystery. It is not only nature that has established the way in which a man expresses himself, his gender, his sexual fate, but also psyche, what I might call, after Jung, his symbolic male predisposition, an "invisible (although based on a visible) nature." Psyche is also nature although we do not often think of it as such. The visible particular is the presence of phallos in/on his body and his drive to use it. The invisible is the constellation of instinctual particulars that constellate around phallos, what people ordinarily designate as masculine personal characteristics, especially, for my purpose in this work, penetration and effectuality.

It is all too easy for a male to judge his sexuality as his burden of original sin, emerging, as he does, from a female who has nothing like his impulse. Over time, the characteristics of penetration, as agency leading to new life, have broadened out from male body as such and have become masculine cultural delineations. When a man acts from instinct with his penis, he not only acts personally, ego obedient to instinct and desire. He also collaborates with male pattern as established by instinct, the result, in Jung's terms, of archetypal presence. A masculine culture develops over time by cumulative male obedience to physical and psychic need. It then balloons out into cultural structure. This is how patriarchy has gained its foot-

---

9 There are two exceptions that I know: Jungian analyst James Wyly's *The Phallic Quest,* which is an exposition on a psychologically important phallic condition, priapism, or masculine inflation, rather than a treatment of the-thing-in-itself, as are Daniélou's and Friedman's works, and *Naked and Erect* by Joel Ryce-Menuhin, also a Jungian analyst who connects phallos with feeling through a psychotherapeutic lens.

hold. Patriarchy takes its form from the pattern of male sexual behavior—intrusion, interruption, invasion. Without potency, this is impossible. Without intrusion, no new life
comes. Yet with intrusion—aggression—as the basis of masculinity, humanity also can suffer, the point of my brief exposition above on shadow. It is a point of this work that male
body form, and the archetype sponsoring it, important as that
is, does not decree male dominance, interpersonally or cultur-
ally.

By approaching masculinity in a radically subjective manner, meaning what a man actually feels and experiences, we
enter the foothills of the mystical. Psyche, as a word, provides a verbal framework for exploring what I might call "the
substance of the invisible," a paradoxical formulation, for substance ordinarily means that which is more material than im-
material. A mystical sensibility is a way for a man to know
himself as he pays attention to what he becomes when psyche's work begins to make demands upon his sensibility. His
response to that which excites him pushes his participation in
the work of manhood, the "four ways" to be discussed here
later. Something new and out-of-mind happens to him. A man
implicitly knows this even though explicitly he may not. He
knows his emerging impulses since he feels them and he wonders about his impending behavior both before and after its
eruption from some strangely unknown, dark interior place.
Following his erotic impulses—as well as his creative and intellectual pursuits—becomes, over time and to a large extent,
a man's touchstone for believing in himself. Psyche is the
means of grasping the surround of soul as soul, like *daimon,*
makes itself felt in his body. Psyche is palpable—one can almost touch psyche, even see and hear psyche, so present and
intimately personal is it, as personal for a man as is his erection. Psyche, and the soul that expresses it, has intentionality.
It is after something. Ego watches it and can learn.

One catches a glimpse of psyche's independence and impo-

sition upon ego—it has a way of imposing itself quite aside
from ego's intentions and even decisions—in the behavior of
phallos. A man's ego cannot order phallos to do this or that,
no matter what a man's culture and religion or law and family
and neighbors decree. Penis erects when psyche is called forth,
when a point of engagement with desire has occurred. Penis,
and the underlying archetypal source of erection, manifests
itself when the psychic base of a man has a need and a hunger,
which the ego cannot effectively satisfy. Desire is hunger,
telling the body of a psychic need. It is soul speaking through
body. Attending to that need is masculine action.

I write this caveat to forewarn the reader that while this
book acknowledges with gratitude both Daniélou's and Friedman's excellent works, I seek to move phallic inquiry into an
area neither of them addresses—mystery: mystery as personal, subjective, soulful erotic male experience. My interest,
to be sure, is more in touch with Daniélou's work since his
orientation is closer to what I as a Jungian might call an archetypal dimension, to what I as a Christian call a spiritual
dimension, to what I as a political liberal call a humane direction. Daniélou's writing reflects a deeply understood and respected transcendent grasp of the male symbol—an attitude I
have entertained in my own works on masculinity. Friedman's
book is, as he states in the title, a cultural history, a valuable
work of scholarship and research, for which I am grateful.

But my interest is different. My interest is a man's desirous
experiences as felt within himself, how those experiences
resonate within and the functional effect they have upon an
individual and his environment. A man who reflects knows
that his masculine body is a strangeness, a mystery that he can
only grasp in wonderment and awe. His ego does not concoct
erection. The awe that comes upon him in desire is ordinarily
projected onto his love object. That she has the darkness and
fascination of the cave, waiting for phallos to enter and insti-
gate life, discovering a hidden place, embroiders his fascina-

tion. He understands himself anew in response to her interest. It begins to dawn upon him that he has the ability to give her what her body and soul need. And through his gift of phallos, it begins to dawn upon him that he has something to give that the family, the nation, the world needs. He is important. None of this is possible without his reflection.

Mystical awareness brings a man not only into an honoring, a worship, an astonishment at the person he loves but also, on reflection, into a capacity to wonder about himself as an agent of creation, necessarily involving his own soul and body expression. He finds in his partner a mirror, a reflection of his own importance, his own sacred workings, the inordinate beauty of that which he has heretofore been willing to assume just belongs, like an arm or a leg. A man becomes proud in the best sense. He does not bring someone else down in order to dominate. He contributes to his lover's importance and to his own.

This work is written as an offering of my explorations into an area many men take for granted, so close is one's gender to the core of a person's reality. Too many men, in my estimation, accept without question the patriarchal suggestion that some part of themselves is suspect and missing if they are not able to live satisfactory lives within a dominating framework and mind-set. (A patriarchal mind-set assumes male gender superiority and expresses an assumption of male supremacy in personal attitude as well as in political and cultural influence.) Such men may question themselves but, unfortunately, not the system within which they live.

I write with an eye trained to find psychic substance in what a man experiences in the deep recesses of his inner life. I concentrate upon viewing masculinity as a mystery and thus the sacramental expression of a man's soul. Since a man's body is holy—"of God," as Quakers say—it requires respect, knowledge and contemplation, as "the outward and visible form of an inward and spiritual grace," as Anglicans say of a sacrament. To designate all that is below the belt as dirty and pagan ignores the beauty and sacredness of body and soul, what makes a man important as a participant in desire and love. Women know what they need. Men must come to know the importance of what they have to give.

Phallos and introspection

The very term phallos, coming as it does from Greek mythological times, suggests mystical and soul presence as well as physical presence. Men discover who they are by means of their gendered bodies and hallmark. They find themselves by becoming aware of what they carry as a male person and by comparison to females. The gender mark that is visible on a male body has its counterpart in a male's unconscious. Every man knows that he is an inner man as well as an outer man. His inner man has a secret, hidden—more often than not, even from his ego—quality about it except when he is offended or turned on. Phallos emerges in expected and unexpected ways. She who sees and "knows"—having it in her hand and in her body—sharing his secret with a man, can be his soul mate. That is why religions place great emphasis upon what men do with phallos. Phallos is not just a means of insemination. Phallos is a primary means of expressing male soul.

Erection—potency—enables a man not only to enter and fecundate the feminine. Erection also provides men an opportunity to find meanings that plunge more deeply into psyche than common patriarchal assumptions about male superiority are keen to suggest. To find those meanings requires an introspective attitude about that which men know well about themselves from personal experience, be it wet dreams at night, masturbation, the presence of erection, the pleasures of lovemaking. Otherwise, any suggestion that a man sacrifice patriarchal dominance will find strong male resistance to change, since no man will willingly surrender what he understands to be the cornerstone of his gender identity without gaining something equally or more important to his self-respect. Every man has a right to feel good about himself. Men need to know that there are positive alternatives to patriarchy.

Introspection based upon phallic mystery begins with self-observation, for a man needs to wonder about what is happening to him in episodes of excitement as well as his long and intense affection and obligation toward his beloved and his progeny. Why does his instrument of urination become hard and anxious? Is phallos appearing on his body a sign that he is entering an archetypal connection with something deeper, something closer to soul? He wonders, "How come I want to do this? How come I want to do that?" "When this?" "When that?" "How can I pull all of this together?" "Am I embarrassed by what I do?" Is it a Divinity that stirs within us? A higher power that requires something of me? Jung wrote of active imagination, a process whereby one enters into a written dialogue with an aspect of oneself in order to investigate the intention of a fantasy figure, really "having it out" with that part of the psyche.

Introspection means to look into oneself. It is difficult to know how a man can release himself from bondage to patriarchal privilege unless he takes his own reality seriously, questions it, kneads it and, yes, celebrates it. *His* reality, not his neighbor's. Should a man fear (as well he might) that he may fall into a narcissistic conundrum of self-importance through such self-examination, let him be aware that contemporary psychoanalytic thinking understands that healthy (not neurotic, as in the myth of Narcissus) self-love is essential for emotional stability. One cannot have clear love for another without a measure of affection and respect for oneself. That "measure of affection" requires a close look at who one is and a respect for that, a tough regard for what one owes and what is owed one. All of these are phallic attributes.

The goal and point of introspection is a personal change in

attitude. A man who habitually looks outward at the world and wonders what the world thinks of him might discover through hard introspection that he kids himself a lot, that he is more interested in his reputation than he is in the condition of his soul. A personal change in attitude almost always is about soul, hidden below a man's customary route, his threshold of awareness. Such an insight escapes him unless he looks within, confronting himself with an intensive kind of caring for himself. A change in attitude, to be psychically significant, must have a wide range of implication and effect—political, hierarchical, emotional, to name a few. Change of attitude can sound banal, obvious, as in a posture. The word attitude has been cheapened in today's everyday culture. It is actually a strong word, indicating fitness, disposition, and indicative of mood or condition. Indeed, Jung thought that a change in personal attitude was the real point of psychoanalysis.[10]

Beginnings

This book began with my presentation of a series of five plenary lectures, collectively entitled *Forced Into Its Nature: Masculine Aggression as a Path to the Soul*, at the Friends' Conference on Religion and Psychology over the Memorial Day weekend in 1995, held at Lebanon Valley College in Annville, Pennsylvania.

I was uneasy about presenting a series of lectures on male sexuality to the Friends' Conference, probably the oldest and most prestigious American Jungian-oriented gathering extant, and I told them so at a preparatory session. "Forced into its nature . . ." is a line from a poem by Sharon Olds, "Greed and Aggression," quoted here later, that I thought supported my take on male sexual ecstasy, forced by body and soul against the puritanical influences of our culture. I expected the conference to be a gathering of spiritually sensitive and, I feared,

---

[10] See, *for instance, Two Essays*, CW 7, par. 252.

quite pious and in many ways proper Christian people, Jungians of a sort though they might be. Quakers have a deserved
reputation for being open, generous, liberal and inquisitive.
But even open people have their limits. They are also products of their culture. Not at all, I was told, "That is why we
invited you."

As I write this now, some ten years' later, I can see my own
fault in what happened at that conference, helped by a discussion of my writing at a recent Scranton dinner party. My use
of the word *aggression* in the conference title and in the title
of this work was the issue at the dinner. I have come to see
that I need to be much clearer—much clearer—in what I mean
to convey. I cannot use *assertion* in place of *aggression* as
was suggested that night—it is a much weaker word and has
little of the importance in psychoanalytic literature that does
aggression. Also I suspect that assertion does not engage men.
Aggression is the issue and it cannot be avoided —it is even
anti-phallic to avoid it. There is a tone about aggression that
is essential to my presentation.

Phallos pushes to insert and assert itself in order to do its
job; it penetrates, it instigates, it intrudes, it is archetypally
aggressive. Even when it is welcomed and beneficial. When it
is not, I fully understand that it can cause terrible damage,
even mayhem, as per my earlier comments above on shadow.

As I presented the concept of aggression at the Friends'
Conference, its full meaning became lost, in spite of my efforts to be careful. *Aggression*, according to the *American
Heritage Dictionary,* means a force that is hostile, an assault.
Aggressive, on the other hand, is defined as having two
meanings, which certainly must be true of aggression as well,
for aggressive is the adjectival form of the noun. One is negative, taking its clue from hostility and in my *Webster,* an invader, emphasizing the imposition of one's will over others.
The second, more positive take is as in assertive: bold, enterprising, active striving, mastery and adaptation. To add to

this, *Roget's Thesaurus* expands aggressive to include adventurousness, venturesomeness, gumption, certainly phallic characteristics. Looked at from that second perspective, aggression takes on the positive, non-hostile tone I associate with phallos and meant to convey in my lectures.

Thus the current reader is alerted to the danger of interpreting my use of the word aggression only in the negative sense, as happened at the conference and at the subsequent dinner party. It is commonly known that phallos can express itself in a hostile manner, causing huge grief in the human community. Such inferior aspects of aggression need attention and they do get much attention in the press and elsewhere. They are not my interest in this work.

I proposed phallos in my Friends'' lectures as an antithesis to patriarchy in three ways: creation, the union of opposites and ecstasy, three of the four ways presented in this book. The three I used at the conference are notions so central to Jungian thought that surely, I thought, in an experienced Jungian setting, they would be accepted as points of departure for understanding masculinity. (Spirit was not then a blink in my conscious eye.) Men at the conference were quite taken with my points but men, at that point in the conference's history, were barely tolerated within its ranks and they knew it. They were glad to have a friend. Women, however, objected to my treatment of masculinity and many did so covertly. A kind of whispering began around luncheon tables and in seminars.

That Jungian-oriented Friends might move so surreptitiously into shadow behavior turned out to be something of a blessing both to me and to the conference, in spite of the difficulty it presented to me personally. The Friends' Conference was started in the post-war 1940s by a German Quaker Jungian therapist from Washington, Elined Kotschnig, who, as I was told, felt that Quakers were so much people of the light that they were hindered in dealing with phenomena of evil.

After the 1995 conference at which I spoke, an ongoing conversation was established by the conference to address internal issues emanating from my presence and the shadow turbulence my topic and I caused. My present writing derives not only from the power of the hostility of those women and their castration threat to me,[11] but also from my need to find a clearer way to express myself. A mystical direction, only hinted at in the Conference, is the way I have found. The Friends' Conference thus set me on a path for a decade, pushing me further into the depths than I could have guessed at the time.

Four ways

In this work I emphasize four ways to delve into masculinity apart from patriarchy: 1) fatherhood, or creation; 2) the union of opposites (the penetration of masculine body into feminine body); 3) ecstasy (male orgasm, or the lifting of the curtain between this world and the other world); and, added since the conference, 4) spirit—the connection between male exposure and risk-taking and phallos—admittedly a bit of a stretch, since there is not so precise a correlation between body-phallos and spirit as there is in the other three ways.

I have added spirit to my Friends' Conference trio of ways for two reasons. One is that by so doing, my "trinity" of phallic elements becomes a quaternity, a notion beloved by Jung and Jungians, including myself, as a number suggesting completion and wholeness. Without a fourth, there is a missing element. That "other" is spirit in this work, traditionally considered a masculine attribute by Jungians, since it is seen to be the oppositional counterpart to matter, which was understood by Jung as archetypally feminine in character. Matter/*materia*/mother are

---

11 I was told by someone who was present at the Conference that in one breakout group a caricature of me was drawn on the blackboard and darts were thrown at it. I could feel the distance from some women, particularly at mealtimes. A problem for me during the Conference was its ritual of keeping silence after lectures, a time when hostile feelings and questions might have been expressed and dealt with.

seen in Jung's writings as being related.[12]

So if matter belongs to the feminine side of life, spirit shifts to the masculine. A reaction, perhaps, and if so, I'm okay with that shift. More and more I can admit that Mother comes first and is therefore primary experientially, perhaps even archetypally, and that masculine apologists must find a way to understand maleness within that context of opposites.

Spirit, however, is difficult to include in a phallic compendium since there is no clearly obvious match between visible and sensory physical erection and spirit as an invisible masculine quality—close to, but not at all the same as, soul. A correspondence between that which is outward and visible and that which is inward and invisible is more easily done in the first three ways, for there can be no traditional fatherhood that we know of without phallos, there can be no genital union of two oppositely gendered bodies without phallos, and there can be no male erotic ecstasy without phallos. A case can be made as to spirit's correlation with phallos, as it will be here anon, but an additional imaginal leap is called for.

The additional imagination, especially regarding spirit but also concerning the first three ways, brings into focus an aspect of psychology almost forgotten today. Modern psychology began as a substratum of philosophy, having to do with the love of wisdom, taking its linguistic meaning from *psyche,* the Greek word for soul. Jung understood this well, as did Freud, however much Freud lacked Jung's original familial religious orientation and Jung's depth of curiosity. Jung and Freud both knew that what they discovered and postulated in psychoanalysis had to do with "a perspective on phenomena."[13] The perspective that psychoanalysis provides could change the way people looked at human life, purpose and motivation—the change of attitude

12 See, for instance, "Psychological Aspects of the Mother Archetype," *The Archetypes and the Collective unconscious,* CW9i, pars. 170, 195).

13 Samuels, Shorter and Plaut, *A Critical Dictionary of Jungian Analysis,* p. 115.

spoken of earlier. Jung was a Romantic, dealing with phenomena primarily from the heart. Freud was a Rationalist, dealing primarily from the head. Each had come across a philosophical construct, the unconscious, which opened the door to a new perspective with the power to broaden ego's boundaries. Freud was first, of course, but Jung, having been introduced to the unconscious by Freud, took the notion into a far deeper realm. For Jung, I believe, it was his loss of fealty to Swiss Reformed Christianity that pushed his investigations into mystery. Freud never had the kind of intense parental/religious influence that Jung did and it showed in the limited dimension of his inquiry and imagination. Freud was Jewish but as far as I know there was no experience of belief in the environment of his family.

Jung's perspective impacts my treatment of masculinity. I find it necessary to look at males from a range that includes inner experience and soul, which is true for a feminine gendered perspective as well. But males have a peculiar way of perceiving, a way inextricably related to the way their male bodies are formed and within which they function, a way implanted by their personal ownership of phallos and the "intention" of the male hormone, testosterone. I cannot discuss masculinity without basing it on masculine body and its plentitude of hormone. But phallos leads me to more than that. Phallos is systemic in men as testosterone finds its way as a dominant into the fabric of male psyche and becomes a way of knowing based on hormonal identity. A secret implanted in the mind and unconscious of a male, working through genetic body, comes to life by means of a powerful sense of masculine body, dominated by a man's personal ownership of phallos as the touchstone of his gender. Only a man can know this as a subjective personal reality.

A brotherhood among men ensues, a spiritual connection based upon their common ownership, their common need and their common heritage. This brotherhood is not based upon patriarchy—domination, an ersatz foundation, based not upon intrinsic masculine nature but upon male politics. Brotherhood leads one directly into metapsychology.

Metapsychology

In order to discuss that which is mystical within the framework of phallos, I tread upon the thin ice of metapsychology, a term which, for me, has to do with the *meaning* of soul-talk and soul-awareness, as in psycho-logy. Metapsychology is not limited to the physical world of the senses however much it finds its basis there. Meta- indicates that which is beyond, transcending, surely the way Jung used psychology. In the ordinary way that psychology is used today, metapsychology has no obvious or immediate place, since psychology is commonly seen as relating primarily to the adjustment troubles people have that lead them into therapy. As I intend metapsychology to be understood, it has to do with the love of wisdom emanating from human experience yet transcending it, circumambulating soul. It has to do with who the therapist is as a thinking and feeling person, what he/she is basing his/her work on in belief and perception and attitude, the fundament from which the therapy is done. And what the therapist is aware of in treating the patient's situation and the unconscious material the patient presents and in dealing with him/herself as a partner in the process of investigation and healing.

Metapsychology extends one's awareness in a nonempirical direction, moving in and through imagination, sensibility, poetry, religion, mystery, parable, intuition, philosophy, literature, politics and metaphor. Metapsychology is nonlinear; it is implicatory, closer to invention and sensibility than to reason. Metapsychologically, one can suggest, ruminate, "get the sense of . . . that which is beyond" behavior—the life of the mind and the soul—the invisible and immeasurable, that which impacts the heart. One cannot prove anything metapsychologically, but once one moves into that mode, one moves into a tone of meaning, into purpose, direction, a larger awareness, a resonance of interiority. Lyricism embeds itself in metapsychology; it qualifies rationality, which must be never very far away, as a song qualifies a feeling. I can say that I love you. The right song might resonate more deeply than the words alone. Love and hate are not defined, per se. They are experienced and told. The mind knows this, of course. But something else, the soul, is the organ that suffers it. Soul is the confirmation of a world beyond ego.

The feminine in the masculine

Also, it must be said that, strangely, both soul and metapsychology have a suggestion of feminine elasticity and mood about them—elasticity, say, as opposed to phallic rigidity, making phallic rigidity effective—and mood, as distinct from and oppositional to rational logos. Rigidity pertains to phallos (it is no good at all as a condition of the vagina) and rigidity is necessary if phallos is to accomplish its biological and psychological purpose as the erect and excited expression of maleness. Logos bespeaks mind as the organ of reason and in contradistinction to feeling, which is often seen as feminine. So one can see how patriarchy stakes its claim: maleness is always rigid and firm, unbending, dominant. That is the box within which the patriarchal mind bounces.

But there is a serious complication. Men are not unidimensional. Vestigial remains of an original, primordial female body-form remain in and on masculine bodies; men are born of females and, as young, are nourished by females; there is no other way. Males share a common human nature with females— they are persons as well as males. No male is only male. Maleness is added to the original structure of the human body by the kick-in of the sex-determining Y chromosome at about the fourth week of fetal development.[14] Before then, all humans-to-be are female.

14 Steve Jones, *Y: The Descent of Men*, p. 6.

And so the paradoxical nature of masculinity deepens. Patriarchy obscures the complicated genetic aspects of masculine development, its assumptions now outmoded by decades of scientific as well as psychological discovery. One would be tempted to call the patriarchy that remains an amusing, were it not so catastrophically hurtful, cultural artifact, a reaction formation, a male defense against the feminine that actually diminishes both men and women. Patriarchy sidetracks men, keeping them from genuine masculine experience as they spend precious time and energy fretting over losses that were never masculine possessions. The fact that men must differentiate themselves, gender-wise and characteristically, from their mother-source, in a way that females need not do, is a great source of the problem. The probability that males, unreflectively trusting in patriarchy, do not find it incumbent upon themselves to seek to grasp fundamentals of their nature and fate as males, is another.

Interior psychic regions that cannot be said to have specific gender reference lean toward the feminine, such as the love and care of children, of art, of receptivity. The thread of connection between masculine and feminine, rent apart by body and soul differences and social conditioning, may have their source in a differential brain development due to hormonal variance. A man can spend precious hours wondering why he is not more open to change, why he may be afraid of adventure, of risk, even as a woman might wonder about a possible partner, a pregnancy. A man may wonder if his fear diminishes his manhood, is a sign that he is lacking in phallic strength. His hesitancy may be the result of a femininity within him, a neediness, a requirement to be cared for. What does a man do with such suspicions? They can lead to a patriarchal defense.

One way to understand such a quandary is to know that no man is all man, that manhood is not equated with patriarchy, with a carefree dominance emanating from his accidental ownership of phallos and testes. The problem is not a man's fault. No such carefree existence exists. Nature itself does not provide an excuse or a way for a male to feel superior to any other being, be it male, female, child, animal or even the hill behind his house, not exactly a being, I grant you, but none-theless a factor of the man's physical and psychological sur-round—an occasion for environmental concern.

Every man has a subjective stake in his female aspects. Every man has a heart, a soul, a passageway into his body —all components of the feminine. Every man can love an-other man. Every man needs to discover his own requirements for living as an equal person and not a superior one, and thus finding and supporting his partner on the basis of his discov-ery. In both psyche and body, for us as humans, there is a need for union with another person, for *coniunctio,* as the alche-mists called it, or, as Jung would have it, a reunion of oppo-sites once together in the distant past, but now separate. The yearning for the restoration of a lost wholeness, masculinity and femininity bound together in a kind of unity, the estab-lishment of a completion, is deeply involved in sexuality and love. What we once were, major traces of which are left upon us, is the metapsychological source of our yearning. We live to repair our brokenness, which is why the attainment of rela-tionship is emotionally necessary for us. A man cannot get to the source of his power unless he embraces a psychology be-yond the boundaries of behavior.

I present four ways of understanding masculinity, its impli-cation and breadth, with a certain delight. My application of these four commonly-used Jungian notions to phallos, and thus to manly definition, has come about through my own struggle with understanding who I am and who my brothers are, aided by my writing of two previously published phallic books, my speaking on the subject perhaps seventy times to university, Jungian and men's groups in North America and in Europe, and my analytic practice—with my gratitude to all the men and women who have spoken honestly and deeply with me in our hours together. And, perhaps most importantly, my placing an attentive ear upon myself.

I suppose that I have come to know myself by observation and wondering, by being a husband and a father and grandfather, in cooperation with a loved and loving woman and by my allegiance to church and liberalism and to Jung. And, I should say, as if it were not by this point obvious, I am aided by my own negative father complex, which undergirds my doubt about patriarchal authority. It has been difficult, but rewarding, to doubt patriarchy and still be glad that I am a man, forcing me to find an alternative paradigm. I think that has happened in me because I have come to know that I am not only a man. I am one-half a human being. I have found, within and beyond myself, that other half. "Half" is too strong a word but I use it to emphasize a point.

For a man to find certain feminine qualities in himself is akin to finding his soul. It is an exciting and enlarging adventure, broadening his capacity to love a woman and enjoy her company as an equal. He no longer feels the same inner compulsion to always be the leader, always have the answer, always know everything, always be right. For a man to be "part feminine" opens humane doors to him, a way to see things other than strict logos permits, to give time, energy, money and imagination to social transformation. That last, social transformation, has a masculine ring to it, but consider the feminine implications of Navy chaplain John Anderson's statement, as he ministers in Iraq: "One of my jobs is to keep men from enjoying war and killing too much . . . to limit the damage in bringing freedom."[15] A man's allowing a contrasexual consciousness to grow in him is essential if he is to move beyond patriarchal domination.

---

15 National Catholic Reporter, July 1, 2005, p. 3.

Again beyond patriarchy; again, four ways

The need for a man to find ways beyond the assumed superiority of and rule by males—to find a new meaning in being masculine—is profoundly exacerbated by the collapse of patriarchy as a dependable psychological and social model. Without patriarchy as a crutch for self-esteem, without a new way for taking intrinsic pride in being male, a man may feel like a ship without a rudder, without a sail even, having no way to propel himself through the rough seas of democracy (one person, one vote— everyone with equal power) and feminism (no male domination of man, woman, child or social organization).

I welcome those onslaughts, for there is no reaching a port without transiting the difficult waters of entry. Almost everything psychologically developmental depends upon perspective and attitude. I believe that every person is equal in essential importance and no one is predetermined to dominate anyone else. There is no divine right of males or husbands— those days are over, if ever they actually existed. A man must find another way to feel and think well of himself and he cannot do so without a knowledge of himself—including his soul.

A man sits at his desk newly limited in what he once took for granted—the pleasure and excitement of play with nearby women, to name only the most obvious. I like to read the comic strip "Sally Forth" by Francesco Marciuliano because it lays out how dumb men can be, how much of the social past men take for granted and cannot find a way around. Or, at his golf club, he moves up to his tee for his round of golf and finds that he must wait for a group of women to tee off. It may be that this man is politically adept enough to hold his tongue and disguise his anger at his loss of preferential treatment. But what happens inside him is the telling point, useless unless he knows himself better than most men do, unless he acknowledges an "inside" that can move into another space, with whom he might have a conversation. A man eats at his table, lies in his bed, and the perceived insult, the terror, of his losing authority and power well up. His need for Viagra, his avoiding looking into his wife's eyes, his search for a new beginning in a regressive direction (new sex, new business), suggests itself to him. Anything, even the ballot box, to help.

How can a man establish himself in a way that enables a refreshed self-respect? My argument assumes that the man will not admit wanting harm to come to anyone, himself included—of course, not always the case, as Jung's concept of shadow amply illustrates and the news tells us daily. It is my contention that a man constricted in uncertainty about his authority is suffering through an uncomfortable but necessary entrance to a new understanding of himself and his world. His old understanding is coming to an end. He needs to look within for authority.

My four ways suggest a paradigm of wholeness as an antidote to patriarchy, as a way of grasping and knowing elements of masculine soul. I write each chapter as something of a personal meditation, sometimes emphasizing but one motif, inviting the reader into my peculiar soul-oriented view. I mean this to be an example of what imagination might introduce into a man's life.

My wife

My wife Barbara is a psychologist. We have been married for forty-four years. I had been a priest long before she knew me and then, for some thirty years, I have also been a Jungian analyst. She moved with me to Zürich twice, pulling our children along, reading Jung and going to lectures at the Jung Institute there, finding an analyst for herself, even interviewing as a candidate for training, in a weaker moment or in a state of high transference with her analyst, which amounts to the same thing.

Jung never was far from our dinner table or our bed, our

parenting, our evaluation of ourselves and others since my interest in Jung began. I might say that Jung—and the mystery of the Eucharist—has dominated our married life to the extent that I dominated our married life. Foolishly I tried to do that and, thank goodness, I failed. I think that failure is a reason why our marriage has lasted so long, but sometimes, even now, my patriarchal remnants veer up like a seemingly dead volcano, making marital survival touch and go, as the story of the dinner party mentioned here earlier might suggest.

Barbara became a psychologist during a two-year hiatus between our two Zürich stints, thinking that such a degree would enable her to train with me on our return to Zürich. Remarkably, it was psychology as taught at Roman Catholic Marywood College (now University) that moved her in a non-Jungian direction. She has a religious attitude and has had one from the start, but one essentially independent of orthodoxies. But she also had and has other consuming interests. Family and mountains have been very important.

This book is not about Barbara, although no work by me on phallos cannot also be about her as my four ways might show. What I have discovered, through the glorious torments of marriage, is that her and my commitments both involve mystery, hers in her way, mine in mine. Sometimes I simply watch us in stupefied wonder, understanding little of even what I think I understand. As I grow older and the sand runs low in my egg-timer, more and more I am filled with an increasingly simple gratitude for what we have had together over our four decades plus. Then I know, within me, that marriage is what the Church calls a sacrament: an outward and visible sign of an inward and spiritual grace, mostly hidden from glancing eyes but deeply embedded in soul.

A soulful attitude usually involves encounter with an explicit mystery, an experience—often surprising—that is far greater than that which ego can design, moving its subject into a condition of reverence, gently nudging reason aside before it gets a serious chance to wreck things. Barbara's connection to the verities is more implicit and naturally introverted, using ego as a means of perceiving strangeness and letting strangeness settle into an overall plan as though it belonged there. (How else could she stay married to me?) As a man ordained, a man trained in Zürich, I have learned as much from Barbara as I have from Jung, probably as much as I have learned from Jesus through the Church. The reverberation of her presence in my life is congruent with what Jung insisted upon as the necessity of inner experience. I write of the four ways with that resonance and that orientation.

Just the other day, for example, she appeared in our kitchen with eyes brimming. She had been reading the reports of six Scranton high school students who had gone, last summer, on Outward Bound excursions paid for by her anonymous "Wilderness Fund" at the Scranton Area Foundation.[16] While I have been, over the years, dashing to analytical appointments and lectures, writing theses and books and talking about them hither and yon, she has been finding her connection with the ultimate in mountains and trails and in our children and grandchildren. She practices psychology but her attitude is much less connected to her ego than is mine.

Gnosis

I have done research on much that writers call mystical and I could repeat here what I have learned from many books and mentors. But rather than repeat what is available aplenty elsewhere, I write of my own experience of *gnosis*—inner intuitive knowledge—and how *gnosis* can be any man's experience of himself were he to have the language, images and *meta*-sense to express what he already knows within in an inchoate way. My four ways are modes of understanding myself

---

16 She is just now letting her guard down somewhat on the "anonymity" issue (I like to think a bit because of my influence).

and my masculinity without being seduced by patriarchy. I do not consider myself in any way an exceptional person, even given my theological and psychological education and experience. I struggle with what inner and personal knowledge and book knowledge that I have so that I might translate what I know into what I speak and write and live.

Education, even experience, *per se,* does not produce *gnosis,* something I tend to think lies at the root of the Foucault quotation at the start of this chapter. It is difficult to say what does. Maybe an ability to feel something happening inside— something that one gradually becomes aware of when one stares at such an everyday phenomenon as pachysandra (see later in this chapter). Maybe at the way one is enabled to see something, or predict something, as one gazes at clouds on a sunny day, as my religiously-deprived mother did in old age two years before she died. Maybe an ability to grasp how it might be that a circle of bread communicates a quality of the sacred and enables one to move beyond the confines of appearance. Maybe an ability to be moved by the example of the late Father Philip Berrigan, pressed to lie down before bulldozers for some forty years to protest the American patriarchal propensity for war.[17]

Common things all, yet mysteries all—strange to a practical man's ears and eyes but actually quite everyday as wonderments. But *gnosis*? I got the courage to claim that when happening upon Walter Percy's phrase, "the holiness of the ordinary."[18] That is a way to catch mystery as I intend it to be understood—not so much in spectacular intrusions of the sacred into everyday life (they indeed are, as the reports of extraordinary mystics testify) but for ordinary people as ordinary evidences of the numinous built into the fabric of every-

---

17 Philip Berrigan and his brother Daniel were (and Daniel still is) Catholic priests who led what was called "the Catholic undeerground" during the Vietnam war. I became a member and participated in one of their actions.

18 See Paul Elie, *The Life You Save May Be Your Own,* p. 428.

day life, since holiness is always present in the commonplace. The walking of Jesus along the dusty roads of Israel, stopping to take a drink, searching out a place to relieve himself, sets the picture: the infinite in the finite.

Males, generally, do not do well with interior experiences of themselves. Oh, maybe some poets and artists do, but usually not ordinary men who must work everyday in ordinary ways to provide bed and board. Think of bricklayers, carpenters, accountants, lawyers. Males are taught, and tend to be, objective, fact-oriented and extroverted, factors that mark one's gender as masculine, analogous to a male's genitalia being "outside" of his body. Little wonder that looking within (since female is "within"—as in womb) does not generally characterize males. Mystical sensitivities in men seem an oddity, exotic, foreign.

Well they might be. But men have a capacity to move beyond stereotypic definitions of masculinity that serve to sustain patriarchal assumptions and thereby sustain the status quo. A man's having a soul penchant—a capacity for *gnosis* as I write of it—is found in his capacity to be inwardly moved by, say, music and art, and admit to it, admit to falling in love, knowing affection and desire for another in a way that no one but the treasured other can quite grasp—and even she may not—admit to having passionate beliefs and loyalties, say, for architecture, farmland, marble, Darwin.

Affairs of the heart or of the mind via the heart, have the quality of *gnosis* when they are markedly separate from the norm, deeply personal, like seizures of commitment and loyalty. When I saw sculptor Bernard Métais's wonderful *La Grande Boucle* ("The Big Loop") on the road to prehistoric caves in the Basque Pyrenées, honoring the Tour de France, I was immediately and deeply delighted by that outrageously exuberant lead cyclist and determined to have it on the cover of this book. Aggressive masculinity, pure phallic energy, was brilliantly caught by Métais as it has been in the imaginations

of legions of admirers of Lance Armstrong, the seven-time
hero of the Tour de France. A powerful zinger about Armstrong is not only his capturing of phallos, transcribed onto a
bicycle, but also his history as a surviving testicular cancer
patient whose disease metastasized into his lung and brain.
The man has become an example of one pushed forward by a
self-knowledge, *gnosis,* that millions of people understand as
stellar and effective, a quality of spirit in the hero.

Personal authority

Personal authority means that a man consciously comes to
know something interiorly via *gnosis.* What he knows is urgently important to his being, as though the man would not be
who he is without it. What he knows is part of his personal
definition, his deviation from the average, his peculiar warp
and woof, the raw material of his individuation in that only he
can know it as he knows it. (Friendship, in this sense, is the
sharing of *gnosis* with another.)

Such knowledge gives a man a sense of strength and power,
sustaining him in his competition with other men, an antidote
for fear and weakness, which all men experience. A sense of
strength and power builds authority. It is phallic. A man with
personal authority does not need to dominate, though he may
need to excel. He needs to be up to the challenges life imposes
upon him, whether they be enormous or small. If he has no
personal authority, a man will substitute an artificial authority
by demanding, bullying, lording. Every man needs validity in
his own eyes. Every man needs to believe in himself. That
which tells a man that he is believable is his soul. He must find
a way to connect with the inner part of himself that he can
respect and love.

Personal authority is every man's private property, the
sense of which is his most important psychological attribute.
A man must lead himself. He can do this only if he listens to
that part of himself who knows, believes what he knows, and

follows his inner core. But the self he follows must be authentic. It cannot be what someone else tells him to do in any ultimate sense. Personal authority is self-generated, as is phallos.

Personal authority has a psychological/spiritual base. Manhood is something more, something additional, to being hormonally male. All men have testosterone, but the "manhood" factor has to do with a personal knowledge and authority that builds upon testosterone and moves toward an explosion, as does his erotic potency, intersecting soul and body, in his interior, mystical realization. He appreciates himself. He senses himself. He enjoys himself. It is his Self that he enjoys. His soul transforms in a way that tradition might encourage but only a highly subjective, soulful experience of Self can deeply legitimize. Such an experience is truth for him.

Michael Polanyi called that subjective condition "personal knowledge." It requires *gnosis,* a secret that only an individual has access to and can metabolize. He finds it in his bed at night, alone or with another.

Initiation

Personal authority in a male comes through initiation. Left to its own devices, nature, in spite of hormonal testosterone, is more kind to and defensive of the feminine and is bent in a feminine direction, since all life is born of a mother and has a tendency to favor its source. Physically, hormones, stemming from genetic decree, establish the shape and function of a gendered body. Psychologically, however, a male youngster, in spite of natural proclivities, must be reared to eventually take his gender identity from men. To do so, he must surrender the protection of his mother, physically and psychologically. That process can cause him to feel that he is bereft, psychically isolated, alone and not-belonging, all accurate. To survive as a man, he must find his own personal authority, his inner core, essential to a firmly anchored masculine life.

Males need to be twice-born and that is what initiation is about.

A male must break from a nature-only process and become, interiorly, as he was physically at birth and before, a person different from his mother. That is a reason why spirit is considered a male attribute. A female is organically in touch with the rhythms of birth. A male is constructed, "erected," not surprisingly. Becoming masculine requires discipline, work and accomplishment. It has a rough and tumble quality about it, quite different from the more organically developing female. Masculinity never develops quietly. It is aggressive, always pushing through boundaries. It is intrinsically muscular and phallically tinged, inspired from within but necessarily dependent upon cultural influences.

After our marriage in 1961, Barbara and I spent three months in Uganda, where I filled in for an instructor on leave at the Buwalasi Anglican theological college near M'bale. Several of my students were absent for something like a week midterm. They were young men, aged about fifteen or so, absent because they were required by tribal custom to undergo ritual circumcision, a cultic entrance into manhood, whereat they dared not even flinch as their foreskin was cut away. They then went into the forest alone for several days, away from their mothers, to meditate upon their new condition. Several men in the class, somewhat older, had missed their circumcision time earlier due to family problems. Once they had missed their tribal ritual, they could not make it up. One, as I recall, had a grandmother die at his appointed time. The men who had missed their initiation appeared to me to be different from the other men—weaker, more pliant, less confident. They learned in class as well as the others; they were kind, almost too kind, and deferential. They were decidedly soft. They had little sinew. Psychic phallos was injured.

I see my Ugandan experience as supporting my contention, though I did not fully grasp the situation then, that a—if not *the* —conduit to masculine soul is through body and ritual connected to body—the ritual being an acknowledgment of soul importance. Knowing one's body and accepting and obeying one's body, treasuring one's body, going through trial regarding body, moving body into wide associations stemming from body configuration means, for a male, knowing and accepting phallos as a way into and as symbol of inner masculine selfhood, or soul. Men who respect adult manhood—and by respect I mean coming to acknowledge and accept penis/phallos/erection as their natural birthright—find themselves enabled to stand with a greater degree of pride, of self-honoring, than they would as uninitiated men. The apogee of initiation is intercourse with a woman, after which a man knows himself in a way that is subjectively incomprehensible beforehand.

Farcical erection—making a joke of it—tells one not much beyond a sort of backhanded acknowledgment of its importance. Nor can a man find himself through timidity or over-sensitivity, which blocks his bravado. A male finds it incumbent upon himself to engage his body in an initiatory way that moves his inner realization of himself to a new place, to be seriously curious about himself and about how his body works, and about the one he desires. Psyche urges him on.

Such is a point of this book as it embraces the mystical. What comes from within and goes out from a male, both physically and psychologically, is of his essence. A man is called upon to respond with his most intimate self if he is not to fall back upon defensive and ersatz self-justification and lashing-out in times of threat. A man challenged by threat, as all men are at some point, needs an inner strength if he is not to feel terrorized, defeated, humiliated or castrated, if he is to find himself worthy of being welcomed by brother males and even more fully endowed by feminine admiration. The feminine, whether inside a male, as anima, or outside as loved one, is a factor of a man's own subjective life and as such is an object of his fascination as well as a complement to himself—to love, to protect, to husband, to procreate, to find pleasure with and enjoy. A man's desire for pleasure shows him what his masculinity, developed as it might be, requires if he is to own his body as his right and feel himself worthy of belonging to the company of brothers.

A gentle, reflective tone of being

The reader will by now know that I espouse a gentle, reflective tone of being, a tone that would not come to a man were he not to reflect upon himself, his feelings, his wonderment at his own body and at the reproductive and erotic products of his body. That, and the wonderment of his partner's body too, and also, in his quiet moments, the wonderment of life itself and how it flows out from his spermatic jets: how life is made, experienced, savored and expanded in what he and his body produce. That is metapsychology.

The point of such reflection for the male reader might be his acknowledging himself in a new way, as a provider of phallic presence, an instigator, a penetrator, a participant in a cosmic drama. Such a discovery, in my lexicon, is mystical, since nothing in the outer world can give a man such a sense of himself as a male—not money, prestige, power or possessions. What a man might find in reflection is terrible in its awesomeness, something quite near the holy, so crucial is his role, so connected is it to the mystery of creation. Having received such a gift, he must know that whatever honor comes his way through his skill in fathering, his qualities as a lover, his attention to spirit, is due to that which he has been given, to what he carries in soul and body, not to his ego management. The power of the unconscious, his inheritance of the mystery, are not entitlements. They come to him from the depths as gifts. A man must work to hone his awareness and smartness. His appropriate response is humility and gratitude, and intense focus, so that his efforts bear fruit.

A man has a need and a right to be proud of himself and his gender; that is, he has a need and a right to self-respect. But self-respect is contingent upon his knowing that his gift carries an obligation. A big part of that obligation is the requirement that he work with his gifts. No matter how many other advantages he has been given or has earned, or how few, a man must prove himself worthy to be a phallos carrier, a contributor to the ongoing life that his maleness provides him the opportunity to express. Being a male can be loads of fun but there is no free lunch. A man's capacity for erection and insemination is an enormous privilege. And there the story only begins.

Reflection

A finely-tuned, seasoned professional analysand, contentedly and gratefully married, once told me that he awoke one night with the urge to urinate but once he stood before his bathroom mirror he found himself wanting to masturbate and to watch himself while so doing. He was shocked at his impulse but he did it. I was not shocked. An intelligent man is also an inquirer, one who knows nothing until he knows it, one who watches himself doing things, both literally and imaginatively, that he would not want others to know about. If he does not know enough, the unconscious will push him toward knowing it. Established boundaries, however much respected, are no final impediment. The capacity a man has within himself to continue to learn—even in the most private ways—is as great a mystery to him as is the seemingly endless wellspring of his body. The wellspring is not endless, of course, but men cannot know that until it happens. My analysand wants to know something as he stands reflected in his mirror, even as it seems to be an accidental opportunity. Reflection is the only way to *gnosis.*

Phallos has a powerful interior resonance for a man, as well as providing exterior carnal knowledge of a partner. It tells a man that he is a man. It may be surprising that a man needs to know this, male genitalia being as obvious as they are, but the omnipresence of patriarchy, and the huge and almost universal male dependence upon it, gives the lie to any easy way of assurance that he qualifies. Revelation seems to be necessary. Men constantly need to prove themselves. Lovers need to know the intensity of body and attraction. When desire— one's own or one's partner's—diminishes or disappears, it needs to be reignited or replaced if a man is to have peace of soul. That the replacement also diminishes or disappears calls forth the need for more reflection. A man needs reassurance that he is a man and he will seek such reassurance in his art, writing, politics, business, family, sports prowess and romantic partners. They can become substitutes for his personal reflection.

Both internal and external knowledge can be mystical, but it is a man's personal and subjective knowledge that I emphasize. Reflection, as with the man looking at himself in the mirror, produces a mode of experience that is psychologically interior, comprehended in a feminine mode, as an opposite observing him, acting as an arcanum, providing a truth about his maleness. As such, the looking and the reflection have an androgynous tone, again an indication of the feminine within the masculine in a tiny capsule of soul and body interaction. The mirror man's personal, subjective *gnosis* was his secret, but it also told him something external about himself, as though the mirror were an other, looking at him. Parts of what he saw he can share, but he can only see parts. He is hindered by his surprise and embarrassment. That does not mean that he is vacant or dense. He wants to share and the mirror provides him with the illusion of sharing. The process tells him something. Most importantly, subjectively, he seeks a new personal knowledge of himself for himself.

I write this page on a hot and wet summer's day. My wife is away at a Pocono hotel visiting an aunt from Arizona. I am

sick of staring at a computer screen and brooding on phallos. I
need a walk. I set out on a short one, like going around the
block except that we live in the country and there are no
blocks. I pass our church which has, next door in a grove of
trees, a burial ground for ashes. I go in there and sit in lovely
shade, thinking of the people I know who are buried there, of
people I don't know who are buried there, of people I have
loved who are buried elsewhere, of my own end and burial,
which can't be too long in the future—but not to be there. I
think of Barbara and what I would do if I outlive her. I touch
my own fragility, my own mortality, my feelings for those I
have lost, for those I might lose; the strangeness of a rich life
that must end in death. I think of our son Steve, flying in
from Hong Kong, due in Scranton at 9:00 p.m. I never used to
worry about flying. Since 9/11, I do. Everyday stuff, but it is
very special everyday stuff. That's what I'm writing about,
"experiences of myself."

What is special is the way one looks, not what one sees in
the burial ground or the pachysandra. Even more, I should say,
is the looking, the noticing, itself. Stuff that is ordinary is usually overlooked. But mystery tells one that what is hidden
within the ordinary is the extraordinary. The Augustinian
scholar Erich Przywara called this "the ultimate transpar-
ency."[19]

Here is another little story. In the summer of 2002, our
five-year-old British grandson, William, was visiting us in
Pennsylvania. Out of the blue he volunteered that the moon
was important to him, that he loved the moon, that he could
look at it for a long time, ponder it almost. He was not at all
so interested in the sun. The sun did not draw his eyes with the
same attraction. What I heard was that the sun had no mystery while the moon was special, that the sun was obvious, not
a sometime glimmer in the night like the moon, and therefore

19 See Tellechea, José Idigoras, *Ignatius of Loyola: The Pilgrim Saint*, p. 581.

less endowed with magic. One could say of course that the moon reflects the sun's light and therefore it *was* the sun that drew him in. Not my point. The idea is that whether it be sun or moon, at the moment of his life about which he told me, William was, indeed, drawn into himself by the exterior moon. An inner connection took place in him, as happened to the man in the bathroom. The subjective aspect of that "drawing in" is what I emphasize as the route to the mystical.

Mystery

Mystery moves one's focus from the outside predominance of, say, the sun, to an inside personal discovery of something that touches soul. It might be that even at his tender age William perceived, in his fascination with the moon, a newly personal sense of himself as one who notices and ponders. But what does that mean? In metapsychological language, William has had an experience of moving into the deeper subjective realms of psyche—far deeper than what we know and treat as ego, which may only notice that the moon is shining. It is important that one catch the resound, the echo. "Into the soul" speaks of an incorporeal, vital core of nature, infusing the body and all material stuff with *élan*. Thus we weep when a loved one is buried or, as in the 9/11 disaster, we realize our loss of innocence as a nation, as a culture. The important element I write of here is that of the *subjective,* one's inner feeling dimension, the radical shift that takes place in one's perception, similar, I am led to suppose, to William's discovery of the power of the moon. Can a five-year-old have that sense of depth? He can. That is important to me as I muse on William's experience, as I consider mystical awareness and masculinity.

Subjectivity

The *American Heritage Dictionary* defines "subjective," in a psychological sense, as "existing only within the experiencer's mind and incapable of external verification." That which is subjective, then, cannot be measured, proved or deliberately replicated. Subjective is, by definition, that which is specific to a person's awareness at a particular point in time, as the definition states, "within the experiencer's mind." That which lives within "the experiencer's mind," or, in my terms, his psyche, is his own knowledge, or *gnosis*. Then the same dictionary goes on to suggest that mystery is "anything that arouses curiosity because it is unexplained, inexplicable or secret." Aha. There it is.

My grandson's fascination had all of those qualities. He knew something. He loved the moon. I listened to him, and it dawns upon me now that his experience is generically what I seek to touch in this writing. The moon is an image. William related to the moon through imagination. Phallos is image. Men relate to it through imagination.

What does that mean? While writing this chapter, I have been reading Anthony Swofford's *Jarhead: A Marine's Chronicle of the Gulf War and Other Battles* (now also a film), given to me by an analysand who was impressed by the book's raw depiction of maleness. So am I. Who knows how much of Swofford's exploits come from an embellishment of his own Gulf War experience in the confines of his writing room—his imagination? What Swofford gives is an unvarnished and rough approximation of Marine life in his own male head and body under the primal conditions of modern enlistment and war. ("It took years for you [sic] to understand that the most complex and dangerous conflicts, the most harrowing operations, and the most deadly wars, occur in the head.")[20] He tells about how it is that males prod one another to be tough even when they only pretend. His words rang true enough to keep me on board out of curiosity about my possible closeness to Swofford and my possible difference from him. I learn about

---

20 *Jarhead,* pp. 247f.

who I am by reading his book, by reverberation, by a certain
excitement in self-discovery; and I learn about who I am not.
He piques my imagination. (The same analysand also pro-
moted the film *Fight Club* which we agreed to watch sepa-
rately, each in our own houses, and then discuss in an analytic
session. In a way, *Fight Club* has a theme similar to *Jarhead*
but the former is really a totally different experience—
violence presented as the means by which men relate and
come close, without questions asked, depicted as a means to
subvert commercial culture—patriarchy—but hugely faulted
by its own superficiality and pyrotechnics.)

Nothing is proved by either my grandson William or Swofford. But I find myself engaged by them both. William was
deep into his oedipal struggle and close to his mother when he
had his moon fantasy. His intuition had not yet been obliter-
ated by patriarchal requirements and prohibitions. He could
still be who he naturally was without much fear of shame, at
least with me. Swofford was way past that childhood condition, yet still deeply enmeshed in innocence as a grown man
and, together with his Marine brothers, needing to prove
something for himself as a justification of his maleness, scared
as hell in war as any kid would be, yet courageous and reflective. Both stories are a kind of poetry, one still naïve, the
other post-naïve but none-the-less naïve as well.

One can see why Jung is so easily dismissed in the modern
world of technological demonstration and extroverted Carte-
sian domination. What threatens the life of the near-adult
catapulted into a political/physical war where the next step is
having one's brains, and with it, one's phallos, blown out is a
society that thrusts men into life and death struggles that they
did not choose. *Fight Club* celebrates that frustration. *Jarhead* judges it.

So when I discuss the subjective nature of mystery, I write
with a sense of deep regret that men today are engaged in ac-
tivities that are phallically destructive but not phallically illu-

minating or redemptive. The only way to that—illumination, redemption—is through one's subjective sensibility.

The pachysandra factor

I remember a day in one of my many weeks' of experiences with the Exercises of Ignatius of Loyola which I undertook at the behest, almost the insistence, of a Jesuit friend, George Schemel, who understood Jung and was a master of the Exercises. I did the Exercises over four years, a week each year, as a guest in Campion Hall, the Jesuit residence at the University of Scranton. Their chapel was an intimate, smallish modern place with foot-high, floor-level windows that ran along two sides, offsetting soaring two-story glass windows behind the altar. I chose my place during my first mass at Campion Hall on my second day, directly opposite where George, and Sr. Judith Roemer, his cohort, sat on that particular day. I was concentrating on Ignatius's idea that God is revealed in all natural things, nothing excluded.

On that morning there was a gentle rain. Outside of the low windows where I sat, I noticed the raindrops falling on the pachysandra in the garden, visible through the floor-level windows. Drops hit one leaf, then another and the leaves responded with a delicate bend and twist here and there and then sprang up again in a kind of dance as the rain trickled off. I was reminded of sitting in my study during my two-book-writing 1989 sabbatical in Zürich, twelve years after my graduation from the Jung Institute there. Daily I looked out over my typewriter from our apartment's large sixth-floor windows toward the pine trees in the garden beyond. Crows would land on one branch, sit awhile, and then fly to another. I wondered, "Why did they leave that branch?" "Why move to that next?" "What went on in that crow's sense of things?"

Something similar occurred to me as my eyes fell on the pachysandra at the Jesuit chapel in Scranton. I became attuned

to the inexplicability of the pachysandra dance. The intercourse between rain and the seemingly insignificant ground-
cover leaves drew me into myself and was suggestive. A soul
response emerged. Was this what Ignatius meant?

My observation of leaf and rain, crow and branch, and the
movement that takes place within me when I notice them
under heightened circumstance, leads me into a way of consid-
ering the mystical aspects of male sexuality. I speak of experience, perhaps my experience, granted, but a man's experience none-the-less, rather than thought, built peg upon peg. I
am not thinking erection, I am having erection, metaphorically . . . erection because I am engaged with imagination as a
love-partner when I am hit by leaf and crow. I am learning
about myself and about the world as my imagination fastens
upon the secrets of nature in a way that suggests penetration,
not dissimilar to the way the body of a woman prompts me. I
have had such experience in erotic explorations as well, always led by the whisperings or shoutings of desire, prompting
me to go beyond where I might be comfortable, where I was
sure of what I was doing or unsure I should be doing it. Once I
followed where desire led, I entered the possibility of *gnosis*.

Desire also led me in the chapel that morning. I was moved
noticing the bobbings of the pachysandra, wondering at their
seeming randomness. accentuated, certainly, by the chapel's
Eucharistic context of sacrament. Being a devotee of the lit-
urgy prompts imagination in me to take flight in any case,
since the rumblings of subjectivity are touched and they open
a door into the source of evocation, the other world of soul.
There is nothing necessarily Eucharistic about either the
plants or my erotic feelings of excitement, yet both point to,
and at the same time demonstrate, mystery. There is nothing
necessarily erotic about pachysandra or birds on trees, but my
finding mystery in the falling drops and the flitting of crows is
not all that different from finding an inner pleasure and revelation in the ritual of bread and wine or in the strangeness and

demanding presence, onrush, of male instinct evidenced by erection. Since mystery occurs to me in those everyday things—I almost wrote tiny, but nothing of this is tiny—it is also to be found in the urgings of my just-as-natural-as-the-pachysandra male body.

Entering into occasions of auspicious similarity or coincidence may be, for most of us, as close as we are likely to come to hands-on occasions of *gnosis.* That is really no problem, for those occasions are enough for an awareness of mystery to slide through the cracks in ego and into awareness. So I have observed in myself (as in pachysandra, as above) and with many men, whose stories, noddings of heads and tyings of tongue I have been privileged to be privy to for thirty years as a Jungian analyst and almost as long before that and even now, as an Anglican priest. Men's sexuality is urgently important to them—but how to think or speak of that importance? It is a hidden and secret and preverbal importance, quite enough to tie a poet's tongue. Sexuality is the primary place where body and soul cooperate, mirror one another, act upon one another, ritualize. Sexuality is a realm of the *numinosum,* divine power, perhaps the main realm, before sublimation and repression begin their work. The language of eros uses touch, seeing, similarity/difference, aesthetics, hope. Erotic numinosity, for men, usually resides objectively in and about the female; subjectively, it resides in himself, as phallos.

The American Catholic, a progressive newspaper, tells me that "biology is stronger than spirituality," a surprising and welcome thing for a Roman Catholic paper to say. The statement is one-sided, but even a half-truth is welcome from such an ordinarily patriarchal source. The sacred always moves both ways—from concrete to symbol and from symbol to concrete. Body cannot be said to always trump spirit meta-psychologically; as I have presented the matter, the reverse is more likely to be the case, however much it might falter or do so erratically in a particular situation. But the statement does point to a growing awareness, even within the Church, of the sacred quality of that which is physical or of the world, subject always to the influence and instigation of the unseen (as in the unconscious and the archetypes). Men would not be men, tied up in soul-body complexities, were there no archetypal intricacies of connection between soul and matter, as in desire being translated into erection, no dependable psychic imprint, as in phallos being the archetypal pattern of masculinity.

Masculinity (in either gender, but here, in this work, in the male) necessarily intersects flesh with non-flesh, as my first analyst Esther Harding wrote in her work, *The I and the Not-I.* What the non-flesh, *the Not-I*—sometimes the Self, sometimes the soul, in Jung's language—requires of the flesh is acknowledgment, which is why men, in pattern, follow and believe in the voice of erection.

Numinosum

What I have been stumbling toward and squeezing out here as I write of that which is radically subjective, embedded in psyche far below the level of ego, is *numinosum.* That which is numinous is autochthonic since it enters one's awareness according to its own laws, something similar to the pachysandra, empowered by its own inherent propensities and rich loam. Ego is the human awareness of the need to survive, to continue to profitably live. That which is autochthonic is apprehended in a radically intrinsic manner, which is why it has a mystical quality about it. Once apprehended, it becomes a way of knowing, *gnosis.* That which gradually becomes known is the *numinosum,* the sacred, the presence of the holy, providing ego with a kind of invisible bedrock upon which it depends in order to function.

Numinosum, as a modern notion, comes from the German theologian Rudolf Otto (1869-1937), expounded in his book *The Idea of the Holy,* from which Jung borrowed much of the terminology concerning what he came to call the Self, mentioned just above, as "a unifying principle within the human psyche occupy[ing] the central position of authority in relation to psychological life and, therefore, the destiny of the individual."[21] That which is numinous in one's experience is responded to with the awe that is the human response to the holy, to the "wholly-other" in the words of Karl Barth.

The *numinosum*, however, is not an arcane and exotic phenomenon, known only by famous mystics. It peeks out at us in our dreams, in fantasy, in art, in our sense of something being very wrong or very right, in the glimpse of an interesting woman walking down the street, in the imaginings of a boy in love with the moon, in one's entrance into a sacred space. We can water that metaphorical pachysandra, that emergence from below the surface, that nudge in the direction of awe, that super, even supra-natural urgency in ourselves, or we can let it wither. Then we get yellow leaves that do not dance. The rain comes down but it is too late and does not reach our roots.

The boy and the crossover point

It is like a boy on the edge puberty lying in his bath and handling his newly larger member, innocent of its powerful ultimate importance. He feels a surge of electricity rising from his feet to his innards and discovers a stream of his inner essence flowing from his member into the bath water. He wonders what is happening. Freud's "pleasure" is not a word for this. Confusion, maybe fear, something precipitously numinous, is closer to the mark. Pleasure may be on the horizon, when he becomes more familiar with the comings and goings of phallos and ejaculation, when he better knows and owns his male hungers and excitements, harbingers of a certain *gnosis*. But that first time, no. He is introduced to a phenomenon and peculiarity of mystery.

21 Samuels et al, *A Critical Dictionary of Jungian Analysis*, p. 185.

All of this is similar to the secret of the pachysandra.

Mystery is the movement from an outside experience into an inside awareness, like a boy's finding a magic in his budding phallos. As well, mystery is the boy's beginning suspicion that his body is a source of discovery, of a movement from the inside to the outside, the power inherent in an intimation of what he might become. Mysticism is the finding of light in the strangeness of such a crossover point, for a crossover point it is, the first time surely, never forgotten, but also every time it occurs subsequently. The inside experience tells him that a kind of screen, a veil, is being lifted, a shade that has hidden his emerging maleness from himself.

In generic "bathtub" experiences, nature finds a way for a male to begin to understand himself and how he is made. It is a way toward which he will ever after seek to find a path of obedience, to find connection with, to cherish and honor, and, if he is close enough to himself, to wonder at. This process is not all that different from that of the alchemists who sought what they needed by trial and error, directed by a mythos which postulated the presence of the *lapus lazuli*, the "gold" of the work, the pearl of great price hidden in the everyday reality of dirt, of ordinariness, of dung—that is to say, a bathtub experience. That is a form of what I see that Jung was after when he opined that neurosis was nature's way of inviting human beings into the mysteries of the unconscious.

A man's erection is autochthonic—emergent from the body's own energy and known, subjectively, by the male as an instrument of his soul. Erection appears to a man independent of his ego; he cannot order it to appear and he cannot easily order it away, although he can modify its appearance somewhat. Sometimes erection presents itself when eros is engaged by the presence of another, sometimes when he is alone, without anyone with whom to share himself or to pour himself into, or even any specific image, internal or external, that excites him. Excitement appears, driven by an inner *daimon,* desire, bidden or unbidden, and appears to a male as *numinosum,* as Jung said of the gods. A man is led to say to himself, "This is me." Such is the core of the male (and, of course, the female, but that is not my story) mystery. Nature pushes itself upon a male but nature cannot totally demand obedience, however much it tries. Ego and the unconscious require cooperation from each other. How a man behaves is another matter and a very important one, but I discuss male mystery here, not morality.

Aggression as intrinsic to males

The aggressive quality in erection is physiologically necessary for phallos to serve its natural purpose to penetrate and to deliver life-producing sperm to a female. The anatomical configuration of the erect penis is designed by evolution to do just that. A few years ago the *New York Times* reported that

the man needs a sufficient axial rigidity so that his penis can penetrate through labia and he has to sustain that in order to have sex. The typical resistance posed by the average vagina is a measurable *two pounds.* The key is to create an erection that doesn't "deform" and collapse when engaging that resistance.[22]

How the writer knows such precise measurements is surely a question, but supposing the accuracy of his claim, or something near to it, an even larger question is why such pressure must be placed upon a female in order for penetration, ejaculation and conception, to say nothing of love and union, to occur. That is not a question this book can begin to address. The point here is that a female body produces resistance, against which the male erection must push. That necessary push is explanation in itself for my use of aggression as an inherent aspect of masculine character, given that phallos is the signifier of masculinity. Hitt's suggestion that "the key is

22 Jack Hitt, "The Second Sexual Revolution," *New York Times,* Feb. 20, 2000, section 6, p. 34 (italics added).

to create an erection" begs the necessary question of how an erection is "created," about which major portions of this book make suggestions (see, in context: autochthonic, ego, soul, instinct). Erections, as already said, well up from the collective unconscious as masculine phenomena; where you have post-pubescent males you have erections. Erections are governed by an inner biological/psychological process the meaning of which I am calling mystic.

The presence of male erotic excitement, heralded by the transformation of limp penis into engaged erection, desirous and ready to perform its function of delivering sperm and engaging the feminine as a desired and necessary object, is the core idea of what I mean in this work by "masculine aggression." To put the matter briefly, male desire emanates from body/psyche's knowledge (*gnosis* is the ancient word for this) that 1) psychologically, a male is incomplete as an individual, that he has need for his outer "other half," as the saying goes. Then, through the prism of evolution, one can also see that erection 2) physically also comes from an inborn male genetic need to reproduce, to extend a man's presence into a further generation, in aid of survival of the species. Erection is a sign that both 1) and 2) are aspects of animal instinct functioning in a male's life. Penetration and orgasm together with the production of sperm are the *sine qua non* of masculine definition and are the body's way of seeking extension and completion, the way back to an original and reunified being, the urperson.[23] A man cannot penetrate without pushing, even in masturbation, where the pushing is simulated. Phallos and psyche are designed and built that way by evolution.

Ergo, aggression. Entering another's body and extending that entering by strong and insistent movement, producing a friction that excites and stimulates a subsequent staunch bra-

---

23 Urperson was the brilliant word-coinage of Alice Petersen, my sometime editor and longtime friend. See Monick, *Castration and Male Rage*, pp. 131f., also below, pp. 115ff. (*ur* in German = origin, source, primeval.)

vado, aimed at climax, is my core image of masculine aggression. Such are the components laid out for a male's erotic soul-path.

These essential aspects of a male's bodily operation have a mystical quality. They rise up from a deep source, which I am calling soul, with no ascertainable help from ego, however much ego might want more power in the arrangement. The aspects "present" themselves, sometimes in quite surprising circumstances, at times welcome, at times not.. They are not, in the strict sense of the word, "intended." They boil up from below as needs, bubbling into the awareness of males with astounding and universal similarity. They provoke the same fantasies, the same dreams, the same delights, the same satisfactions, the same desires, driven by the same four ways, in males everywhere. This may be attributed to an archetypal presence in the psyche, formed by aeons of repetition.

It might be well to consider that aggression makes no real sense to liberal folk unless it be considered as an opposite to that which is passive (receiving) and organically waiting to be brought into being. That which "waits" has little self-ability to come alive on its own; it needs another, an insertion into its waiting reality, a prompter. For the waiting feminine to come into fruition requires an active contribution from beyond itself. That is the phallic contribution. Both genders are always *in potentia,* the feminine waiting for masculine fertilization, the masculine yearning for feminine conception, in aid of which comes desire to enliven and stimulate his erotic imagination. Activation is the masculine issue. The dance of lovemaking, particularly male leading, with all of its gyroscopic twists and turns, reflects universal male piloting and one that inevitably follows an aggressive course. A male's hungry need for the actualization of a below-the-surface life energy, so that he might do what he was made able to do, constantly impinges upon him by the unconscious. His need actualizes his fate.

A man's limited span of potent aggression, profoundly felt in his riper years, exacerbates the situation. A man grows older yet the unconscious seems to know nothing of age. It keeps feeding him erotic signals long after they make logical sense or he can do anything about them. Rapture, a sign of the end in Christian eschatology, is the movement from a placid state to a heavenly one, glowers at him from around the bend. It may be, I sometimes think, that rapture in Christian Biblical sources, particularly the Book of Revelation, is a compensation for the failing of human erotic capacity, especially masculine capacity, since the scriptural books were unfailingly written by men. Erotic rapture may be a foretaste of the Kingdom. Certainly Bernini's sculpture of St. Theresa of Avila in Rome leaves that impression.

Soul markings

Roget's Thesaurus defines "intrinsic" as that which is fundamental, as inner-ness, as essentiality, as core, as foundational. So when I write about intrinsic maleness, I suggest "that-without-which" elements, elemental components which lead a man to a grasp of the importance of his masculinity. Deeply embedded within a male's psyche/body is his need to be important to women, especially to the woman he loves. How a man's soul is marked by his loving and being loved, how he is changed by his stroke of luck, his happenchance meeting, his missing the boat, his right and wrong choosings, her loyalty and her deviousness, can tell the tale of his life.

When I muse on soul markings, I think of the old American midwestern stories of the Norwegian farmhand notching his belt for each woman he has enjoyed, as a corollary. Soul deepens and changes with the quality, and, yes, the quantity of adapted skill, always a test of potency. The intrinsic qualities of phallos have permutations throughout a man's life, far beyond the literalness of erection but metaphorically derivative of erection: hard, intentional, insistent. Such "soul markings" give a man the means for understanding the "why" of himself and the "overplus of meaning," in Rudolf Otto's words, that surrounds his gender talisman.[24] The marks are present in every post-adolescent male whether or not he recognizes them or consciously "gets" them.

To me, "soul markings" add a masculine nuance to the common Jungian notion that the soulful aspect of a male, his anima, necessarily has an overarching feminine quality and tone. I have heretofore used that idea in this book; it has a logic and reasonableness to it, an "on-the-mark" quality that I accept. But it is not the whole story. It may indeed be a quite mischievous notion that a man's tender places, his deep feeling and his inner mystical truth are, by definition, always qualities of his repressed opposite sexuality and not of his own authentic nature as a male. But there are aspects of phallos that are excruciatingly sensitive while continuing to be clearly masculine. There is, of course, an important truth to Jung's idea that the anima is an inner contrasexual aspect in a male, leading him into the maternal unconscious and foreign aspects of himself, as psychopomp, having a feminine face and attraction. A man's masculine soul is brought alive by her milky opposite desirability. There is a distinct limit to a man's ego leadership and here is one of them. But a man will first, before listening to anima, follow his natural bent and the mystery of his own interior workings.

Irene Claremont de Castillejo was a great teacher of mine—if but by reading. She was the first Jungian I'd read who seriously disagreed with what I then considered to be Jungian orthodoxy. She wrote that a woman's intelligence cannot be understood simply as (masculine) animus, and, even more surprising to me then, that a woman's soul is feminine, not masculine. Females have minds that are genuinely female, that belong to them without our needing to borrow from the mas-

---

24 *Idea of the Holy*, p. 5.

culine logos in order to understand them. De Castillejo taught me that inner masculine essence also has an authentic nature that need not be reduced to its opposite.

Just after re-writing this section, I had an analytic hour with a man who is an accomplished international abstract painter. We were discussing his approaching exhibition in Munich, why he paints, how he experiences and how he perceives. He spoke of his "marking" his work as a way he knows its completion, as when he can stop re-doing, re-touching, re-working a piece. Marking means the piece is ready to go out from his studio. He said, "I allow myself to think that my marking is important. When you depict, you draw. When you mark, you evoke. I bear witness. I think of bearing witness as not being judgmental."

El Chuchumbe and Dionysos

A good friend, Judith Gleason of New York, a Jungian psychotherapist amongst her other many talents, makes remarkable videotape documentaries of indigenous peoples in Mexico. Recently she sent me her latest ethnographic video, "Sentinels of the Earth," showing the people ("Popoluca") of the region of Soteapan in the Sierra de Santa Martin area, far south on the Gulf of Mexico coast some 120 kilometers below the city of Veracruz in the Veracruz state. I watched episode after episode of her filming of those valorous people, torn from their roots by patriarchal dominance, 56% of whom are illiterate, until the final sequence came on, hitting me over the head with a bat.

On screen were three young men, the Arizmendi brothers, early to late teenagers, who taught themselves to make and play guitars in order to revive old songs of the Popoluca for their enrichment and to save their heritage in a time of cultural decimation. It was the segment on El Chuchumbe and the boys' song about it, as well as a previous song, El Guapo, roughly translated on screen, which blew me away. These young guys were singing about the mystical aspects of male sexuality, in rough vernacular to be sure, very close to what I labor to write about. I am separated from folk wisdom and I must make something of a head connection with that which is both natural and intuitive for people who live less in their intellect. They sing openly, unselfconsciously and joyously.

El Chuchumbe is, in my Jungian words, a term for the archetypal phenomenon of male sexual energy. It is the erection, emerging in its natural form and in masculine pronouncement and action and, for these young men, its numinosity. In her "Program Notes" for the video, Gleason calls El Chuchumbe "a song on a Dionysian theme . . . a regional personification of a humorously magical 'sex drive,' " and more: "The touch of the Chuchumbe will enchant you . . . You can't avoid sudden possession by your personal Chuchumbe." Sex is always funny as well as diabolical, since it comes into our lives in unexpected visitations, quite at odds with propriety, whether primitive or encultured. That quality substantiates sexuality as being mystical. Rational efforts to describe it fail. It requires humor and song and, to be grasped, a capacity for wonder.

Dionysos, and a valuing of his place in mystical sexuality, continues to be suspect in proper psychological circles, Jungian as well as elsewhere. He is hardly ever seriously considered in treatments of male sexuality, an omission that speaks volumes about conventional American, British and European propensities. In spite of our modern Western outbreak of sexual freedom, surely Dionysian to its core, even those at the highest levels of psychological and mythological accomplishment are wary, even afraid, of Dionysos. He is an irrational phallic god whose predilections jump directly from the unconscious into outrageous behavior—whatever moralistic or rational interference there may be in a man do not come from Dionysos. He is part of everyman although, of course, some men find his mad dispositions more part of themselves than others—but I would say that every man is Dionysian at the point of orgasm. He becomes rather insanely immoderate for and with penetration, his impulsiveness pressing for release into unrestrained delight and danger.

Dionysos deserves respect as well as caution, for valid aspects of the unconscious do not know or obey the restraints of ego and society. But fear and avoidance undoubtedly build the power of that which is forbidden and certainly the uncivilized intrusions of Dionysos.

Yea, but avoidance leads nowhere in unraveling the mystical aspects of male sexuality. El Chuchumbe and the song in his honor (I say "his" since I am pressed to believe, in collusion with Judith Gleason's notes, that the "humorous sex drive" she writes of is essentially masculine) bespeaks the absurd irrational influence of erection and the sperm behind it demanding liberation, plunging out helter-skelter from phallos in mindless fountains. Humor takes its cue from the strange protuberance extending from the trunk of a man's body, especially so from beneath the skirts of the pretentious priest in the boys' song, demanding attention in an adolescent and narcissistic way. Dionysos seems quite foolish even as the most ordinary acts of erotic love seem intensely embarrassing to the rational daylight mind, which is why they are generally undertaken under cover of darkness, with the aid of music, food, drugs, alcohol, suggestive lighting and other environmental assistance.

El Chuchumbe plays a part as well in every female as a more-or-less recessive psychological phallic presence. To Jungians, this is her animus—her mind, her demanding quality, her authoritative opinions; to Freudians, her exhibitionistic presentation, found in makeup, hairdo, cleavage exposure, stylish dress and personality insistence—her aggressive exhibition. Be whatever it may, the contrasexual phenomenon in a woman naturally finds its source in the emergent insistence of phallos, a suggestion, an overtone, of her gender opposite. In and of herself, the feminine teases phallos out of a man, plays with it, celebrates it in the male-female dance omnipresent in love making.

Everyday eyes and ears

Just this Sunday morning, as I write this, I sit remembering how it was that at Eucharist my eyes fell upon an attractive woman sitting in her pew, someone I know but not well and had not seen for months and missed, accompanied by her handsome male friend. I might say that I penetrated her with my insistent and grateful gaze. We danced for a moment as she returned the look. I was glad to give and she seemed glad to receive. I then got out of the church quickly. That moment was why I went to service this morning but it was not why I went to church this morning.

My perspective on the mystical aspects of masculinity might take its clue from hundreds of quotable words from Jung, none of which have any direct connection with masculinity per se, but all of which might apply to my theme. They wouldn't need to directly refer to symbolic erection any more than pachysandra or crows or a boy looking at the moon or a boy in the bathtub has any necessary connection with the mystical. Mysticism is an interior way of looking at life, a way of seeking when one knows that "answers" are no longer the answer. Of course, answers are still sometimes answers, but what requires attention, for one moving in a mystical direction, is what the soul needs and what the soul says and what the soul catches on to.

How one can practice that without falling into New-Ageism or piety or romanticism is an important question. I suspect that one way is just to stay quiet a lot of the time: to read, yes; to listen, yes; to stare at the wall or growing things with nothing specific in mind; but not to enter into disputes as if one were trying to win or make an impression. And to say less and less all the time, especially when the conversation is soul-less. To just get away from the noise, or as one friend who is working to establish a spiritual retreat practice has put it in his promotions: "Turn Down the Radio."

That was Jung's way of looking, or so I suspect, and the Jesuit George and his Ignatian way of looking, and more and more, as I grow old, my way of looking. Mystery is taken with a new kind of seriousness, the more so as more about life, looked at by ego, seems banal, but looked at by soul is laden with nuance and mystery. A new capacity for wonder—especially since 9/11—emerges in me from my center, much to my surprise and, sometimes, discomfort. Jesuit George didn't seem all that surprised and he urged me to take "the mystic" seriously, which I thought at the time was an off-the-wall suggestion. It is essentially irrelevant whether or not any of my other teachers or analysts saw my emerging everyday mystical orientation as I now see it. George did. He put the notion of the mystic out as a hook in our talks about Ignatius, and I, the fish, over a period of time, kept nipping at it. I have a suspicion that he wanted to convert me, already an Anglican Catholic, into a Roman Catholic. He wasn't able to do that. But I had a new model on which to hang an obscure and vague sense of myself that notices, listens to and wants to respect "the overplus of meaning" surrounding me with an inkling of awe, from a too-obscure place, a deeper place, a not-out-there place. Surface reality continues to be surface reality but it becomes only part of what one sees.

Mysterium tremendum

In "The Symbolic Life," Jung writes of the esoteric and alchemical *mysterium tremendum*, that which "reaches down into the history of the human mind" into a prehistory that is "the expression of a fundamental psychological condition."[25]

---

25 *The Symbolic Life*, CW 18, pars. 616f.

As opposed to the language of ego and modern rationality, which is the *lingua franca* of the otherwise excellent treatment of penis by Friedman, Jung posited his work on what occurred to him, welled up, as he listened, read and studied, concluding that "only the symbolic life can express the need of the soul."[26]

The symbolic life emerges from the unconscious into consciousness. There is no way for the mind to totally grasp symbol—that is the point of symbol. But according to Jung, the mind must give in to it and respect it, in a feminine way, which for a man requires a radical transformation of attitude. That is the mystical alternative to reason.

Jung saw life as divine drama, elevating its ordinary elements to sacramental importance and bringing the sacred down from a lofty perch into one's living room, or, as Robert Calasso has put it, "bed is the primordial place for excellence."[27] Without such a visionary imagination, penis remains banal and cannot reach its symbolic capability to become phallos. The problem with modern man, Jung wrote, is not neurosis but his "terrific fear of loneliness."[28] That loneliness is life without a connection to soul, when one does not know, ignores, dismisses soul.[29] The religious life, which Jung described as "the life of the careful observer,"[30] is involved in a man's noticing the data parading before and beneath the ego, the stuff that moves him, including an observation of himself observing a wide variety of human vision and experience, not just those approved by collective opinion or teaching. Everything human, past and present, is data. Religion is "not an opinion," writes Jung, it is "an absolute

---

26 Ibid., par. 627.

27 *The Marriage of Cadmus and Harmony*, p. 24.

28 "The Symbolic Life," *The Symbolic Life*, CW 18, par. 632.

29 Ibid., par. 633.

30 Ibid., par. 673.

experience" which "cannot be discussed"; that is, argued about.[31]

In that sense, my notice of the pachysandra in the chapel, when soul saw something in the leaves and rain, can be seen as a religious, symbolic moment since it came within the context of "the careful observation of data," the important qualifier being "careful," which means to me that one looks at data with the subjective resonance of soul. Ergo, one must, at least sometimes, be contemplative when one looks . . . not in a hurry, strongly focused, with an ancillary awareness of "an absolute experience" being possible, even likely, even present, in the looking. One must be prepared to see something beyond sensory data, something of the presence of the mystical, when one looks. Jung does not tell us what we are to see when we observe, or what the absolute is, but only that within "the careful observation of data" lies the human potential of soul perception, leaving a door quite open for a wide variation of meaning within a religious context, which is to say, in my words, a soul context.

Jung tells us, also in my words, to take the time to look and then to catch the resonance, the interior tone, of what we see, to let it have an interior effect upon us, reaching beneath our common use of rationality, allowing what we see to influence our awareness, opening us to the radiance of mystic insight. And, importantly, to pay as little attention as possible to what others think of *what* we see. This cannot be done unless we be quiet and look within for authority, and trust that authority, stepping into an other-worldly ambiance, a condition where we have some hope of being in touch with what Harding called the Not-I, that which the ego ordinarily overlooks. Usually, we become so overwhelmed by extroverted stimulation that we hardly notice, or worse, shrug off the tremulous quivers of soul within us.

Ask a man who has an erection, "What is going on with you?" and you will likely be told of the object of his affection, of his desire, if you are told anything at all. You will be told

---

31 Ibid., par. 692.

nothing of what he subjectively experiences, of what soul contact has brought his masculinity out front. There is no easy way
to talk about it. Yet that is what I have come to believe Jungian
analysis is most importantly about—the increasing desire to
speak of one's soul loneliness, loneliness in the sense of "seeing"
what others rarely see, to say nothing of mentioning. Soul
articulation can lead one to dry wells, even worse, into the
wellsprings of despair, into a loneliness we are afraid can never
be healed, into John of the Cross's *Dark Night of the Soul,* into
knowledge of a need the gratification of which we fear can never
be found. What soul articulation promises is a reflective touchstone in those dark depths, without which the light, when and if
it comes, has no opposition. And a sense that one is at last upon
a path of reflection.

I have come to believe that no man has an erection without
soul involvement and the presence of *mysterium.* The appearance of a man's erection is a sure sign of his masculine soul's
engagement; it is masculine soul's articulation. A physical erection is not a mature man's only soul articulation. For many,
their life accomplishments become metaphors for erection. But
erection might be the only soul articulation for a desperate man,
a man without the resources of sublimation or a man caught on
the cusp of not so much personal loneliness but of existential
loneliness, of angst, of a sense that life goes nowhere and is
meaningless. That is the loneliness of which Jung wrote. There
is no clear role for that man to play in the cosmic drama, in the
meaning of life, as the American Indians understood their worship of the sun as ensuring another day of existence. I suspect
that angst is what many American men are finding in themselves, however deeply buried, after 9/11. Certainly I am enmeshed in something of that, which is a reason why, after visiting Ground Zero, a month after the fact, I fell into uncontrolla-
ble shaking and had to be taken to a hospital where the doctors
suspected that I had encountered a virus on site. Faith in American invulnerability and superiority, even when it was not iron

clad, as mine was not, was undone whether consciously or unconsciously in that event and in its implications for the future. Anyone can walk into a terminal or drive onto a bridge or into a tunnel with an explosive device in the trunk. The formulas are on the internet. The end of life as we know it can be hidden in the sole of a shoe.

The body and its wonders is an enormous storehouse of energy and meaning. For females, the wonders are celebrated and openly observed in spite of feminine interiority—one cannot mistake a well-along pregnant woman as she appears before the eyes. A man's external wonder is hidden and secret, exposed only to a loved or desired one, someone who might be willing to take phallos in. Males have compensated for this by constructing patriarchy, outer political-phallic domination, which, however phony, propagates and practices masculine superiority. Many of us hope and work for a new democratic time and wonder what to do with what we observe and experience in the present. Jung might advise us to continue observing the data and developing within ourselves some sense of what we see and some intelligible plan for the future. Involved in this observing is the need we have to pay careful attention to the interior joys and pains that we suffer, that we might begin to let go of the old way we know so well and practice so often unconsciously. Then we may begin to know the way of *the* mystery and our mystery.

For men in their nakedness as males, the mystery begins with a respect for the fundament that makes us men.

Four ways of masculinity, yet again, and the garden

In the following chapters of this book, I address each of four mystical aspects of masculinity. These ways do not cover all the possibilities. But in order to flesh out each mystery, in a short book, I must limit myself.

I have a meditation garden in my Pennsylvania acre. The stone wall around the garden, about the size of the collapsing barn at which place the garden was built, is the limit of the garden. Everything in the garden grows within the square marked by those four walls—their containment, their bounds, their guardianship. The walk into the garden begins at the gate, two stone pillars that suggest phallos. Those walls and the pillars suggest the masculine propensity to engender, define, value and limit.

The stone walk in the garden is in the form of a question mark. Entering the garden, one winds around the curve of the question mark to the center, obscured by tall cypress trees, until one reaches the vortex, where a tall feminine beaux-arts marble statue stands opposite a meditation bench. A secret is revealed. She is the nucleus; the masculine protects her and the entrance to her presence. One enters, also masculine. Then one finds. Ergo:

> Creation/Fatherhood
> Union of opposites
> Ecstasy
> Spirit

2
Creation/Fatherhood

Creation, in the sense that I use the word here, means fatherhood. Phallos is inseparable from the making of new life. A
male's participation in creation makes him a father.

The primal urge a male has to become a father has its origin
in two things:

1. Ancestral (archetypal) heredity, psychologically considered. This is a consideration based in the past.

2. The evolutionary impulse in males, common to all men, to
pass genes to another generation, thereby extending life and
influence into the future.

Looking Back

No man knows how to be a father when he first becomes one—
and probably not for a long time thereafter. A male's sexual interest comes upon him gradually in adolescence and if he is true
to himself and courageous and no impediments stand in his way,
he acts upon it. If his seed hits its mark, and ordinarily only one
of millions he ejaculates does so, he becomes entangled in the
beginnings of a life-long fatherhood that is beyond his ability to
fathom, in his erotic press, at the start. Only years later, if he
has embraced a modicum of responsibility in exercising his sexual
desire, in caring for his progeny, will he begin to comprehend
what he has done and what a wonder it is, he is, and his young
(and their young) are.

I was a son, needing, as I grew older, to separate myself from
my father, to go my separate way. Then, suddenly, or so it now
seems to me, I was thirty-two years old and I became a father
less than a year after marriage, which seemed pretty sudden to
me. Barbara looked at me incredulously, as she has so often in

our marriage, when I brought a television set into her hospital room so that we could watch the Johnson-Goldwater election returns on the night after Kate, our second and final child, was born in 1964. I thought that nothing could be more important than Johnson's defeating Goldwater. That was not her idea at all. Of such is the story of our marriage. I was ahead in "major" things, like God and Jung and the Democratic Party, once I had made my switch. She was ahead in "minor" things, like family and children and the outdoors. Over a long time I painfully discovered that the major and the minor often had to be reversed.

In being conscious of the importance of my fatherhood at the time, I was retarded. I took it for granted. Child-consciousness was a woman's job. I could not take for granted my being a father in the Church but I did in our family. I had to learn in marriage what Barbara had brought to the marriage.

Of course I had ideas about fatherhood in my earlier years but I was not itching for their achievement. What was paramount was my life as a priest, a public figure far different from my Masonic lawyer father, who, even though he held political office, responsible and honest as he was, was never a particularly vigorous public figure. Now, looking back, I can see the rivulets of his ethical influence that formed the background of my decision for ordination, though that direction seemed incomprehensible to him at the time. I did not know my father either well or personally. He did not expose himself easily, even hardly at all. I recall once, when I was planning a trip to Chicago, the big city to us at that time, he handed me some money, telling me to "have a good time." I have wondered since whether he meant that I should find a girl or buy a few drinks. Those were days when I could not have imagined my teetotaling, moralistic father suggesting either of them. But I have not forgotten his strange offer. Was he revealing something to me in money code?

It seems to me that I had to find a path for myself, not in a way that reflected what a father might fulsomely give to a son. He assiduously kept his hands off. However, I did watch him and learn, if but sideways. The subterranean connection of father and son, when not intimate, takes its power from what behavior the son notices, from their common genetics physically and their archetypal heredity, psychologically. I suspect that I would have both of the latter in the texture of my psyche had I never known my father—I would still carry his genes and his maleness. That, itself, comes upon me as a mystery. He inhabited our home as a semistranger, as one who did not quite allow himself to belong. He handed the family to my mother.

Knowing my father in a somewhat mystical way might have shown in my nodding of head when I first came upon Jung's writings about archetype—a universal pattern of life stretching backward in time yet showing itself in secretive ways; the pattern emerges from within without any cooperation from conscious intention. I knew the man from his proximity; I sensed something of him, like the time early one day, when I was maybe six or seven, he came early into my room dressed in golfing clothes. I had no image of my father as a golfer. His appearance was incomprehensible to me, like someone unknown who had walked in off the street on a lovely June morning. He was introducing something in himself to me—which he inexplicably did from time to time. I now suspect that it was his need, in spite of himself, to be known by me, the emergence of an archetypal requirement that he pass something of himself on, an inference of his phallic identity. He was "my creator" and I suspect that he wanted to reveal something elemental about himself, like the possibility of his being other than a provider, other than a public servant.

What I may have sensed in him was something of a pattern of fathering which he ordinarily disguised or, at least, did not easily display. Why my father would disguise his fatherhood has been a question for me throughout my life, and it may be a reason why I write this book. For it is in the nature of an ancestor to give to the young—and even to the old—a pattern of emulation, an introduction and, at best, a gentle guide, to the secrets of what lies ahead. I remember well two of his sisters, reasonably intelligent women, coming to our house at election time bringing facsimile ballots for him to mark so that they would know how to vote.

Jung's archetypal thinking suggests that a primal pattern in life is inevitably present, however faint it may seem. One catches a glimpse—often only a glimpse—of the pattern *sub rosa*—as it flashes by disguised in the obvious, often unremarkable at the time, strangely remembered decades later. Pattern in psyche is as present in daily life as is, say, two arms, two legs., easily missed in the apparent, yet present, having been built into the psychic (genetic) pattern of life for eons. Male parenthood, fathering, has a pattern. It is essentially similar—and essential—in and to men everywhere, however it may vary in particulars. Whether it be judged good or bad in one's life experience is basically irrelevant to my discussion here. Fatherhood is present in the background of everyone's general realization. It is known and expected even when it is experientially faint.

Erection is a natural masculine occurrence, an important part of the archetypal pattern. No fathering takes place without it and its implications. Erection is present in all fatherly authority, taking its cue from the behavior of phallos in conception. Even though sexual phallos is hidden to all but one's partner, beneath the cloak of propriety and morality, the metaphorical extension of phallos into fatherly attention, instruction and care should not be. Fatherly affection and pride, honestly and happily offered, is an enormous asset to a child, and to a son it can make the difference between a so-so beginning and a strong one. But a father who is insecure himself, or ignorant, or selfish, avoiding his phallic responsibility and sidestepping the obligations of his pleasure, can miss the boat. Or worse, distort the journey itself by taking refuge in obvious or oblique patriarchal attitudes and demands, diminishing his son's incipient authority or forcing it into antisocial directions. Patriarchy is a powerful substitute for an open acknowledgment of phallic/fatherly strength.

Looking forward

A man lives with the creative implication of erection every time
excitement comes upon him, suggesting, mystically and by extension, his own father potential. The necessity of father in the
family is a way of speaking of the pattern of archetype. It would
be a more conscious world were boys and men more aware of
their symbolic as well as their physical importance in begetting
new life. But whether they are aware or not does not change the
situation. Erection is the harbinger, the announcement, of archetypal father presence on the horizon.

Let me step more deeply into the mystery of fatherhood. A
male on the cusp of his father potential finds himself entering a
radically new expression of himself. He may shy away from the
loss of more carefree living but, should he be enough aware of
himself and his part in life's mystery, he also feels a budding
pride in becoming a desired and needed person in a startlingly
new way. He stands poised to participate in the great chain of
being and will do so due to the importance of his phallic presence
and its contribution to his attractiveness. What is this, his new
pull, his new appeal? Why is he suddenly noticed by someone
when before he was just another guy on the block? Something
emanates from him, a new power I here call potency, almost
totally absent before his pubescence. This is his introduction to
masculine soul, the interior realization of his change and his new
value.

In Jungian parlance, this is a male's father *imago* prompting
him to go on with himself, urging him to come alive to his own
life potential, to begin the process of obedience to the archetype
of the father emerging from the depths to claim him. He is
beckoned to accept this destiny, in small shyly and slyly kissing
steps to be sure, but gradually to go on to the main event, allowing and embracing and offering his masculine reality. He
comes to learn that his sexual maturation is the speech of his
body, and, in his beginning awareness, the voice of his soul. He

needs to go through this transformation. A young man's genes direct his interest to procreating another generation, which he begins by his adolescent playing around. He is ignorant of this, but nature ignores his ignorance. His early ripeness impinges on his awareness as erotic intensity, the need to penetrate and explode—there is little mental directedness in the matter, unless the youth is hindered by convention. Young men are driven; every sports page tells us that. They hardly ever engage in sex because they consciously want to become fathers. They are pressed by their instinctual energy, the archetypal force within that confuses everything that previously seemed so simple. What begins in puberty never leaves a man, bespeaking the importance of his early family life. He may become old and tired but the power of masculine identity remains, even if vestigial and in shadow. It is something he knows about being a man.

Fatherhood brings enormous obligations. A man must pay for the pleasure of sex and company, of friendship, of helpmate, of her desired return, as too must a woman. The list of bills due, requiring his labor, never ends. The anguish of disappointments in a wife's vacillating erotic interest, the complications in his child's life, his own wandering interests, never end. I remember meeting a single priest friend walking down the street in New York on a Saturday morning when my children were very young. He was on his way to Bloomingdale's for a morning of recreational shopping. I thought, "You are going shopping?!?" I had to take my kids to the park. (Shopping was no recreation for me—but he had the freedom to make that choice and I did not.)

Fatherhood also brings enormous pleasures. Small ones romping through the house, taking them to school, hand in hand, their lives beginning anew each day. There is the pleasure of being responsible for a son who needs a father to be responsible, as when I spoke to our son about the impossibility of his being involved in selling drugs at his boarding school, no matter how much he craved the money and importance, no matter how much he liked the kid who stole the drugs from his doctor grandfather. There is the pleasure-pain of father-angst in looking for a child who is lost in Central Park and the indescribable joy in finding her patiently waiting to be found on a park bench. Or the maddening anxiety I felt for that same daughter as a teenager, out late at night, and the relief in her coming home safely after my scouring the country roads, daft with worry. There is the pleasure of buying a book that the child would love even if it is never read, found years later with the back still unbroken. There is the pleasure of graduations, visits to one's offspring's home in his or her adulthood, noticing the similarities to one's own home though never a word of instruction had been given. There is the pleasure of grandchildren and the satisfaction that a daughter who lives in London and a son in Hong Kong like to have us visit. Ordinary things, yet crucially important things—that give us joy since they carry archetypal weight.

Immediate fatherhood falls into the background of an aging man's consciousness but it never disappears. Archetypes do not disappear—they merge into the fabric of the everyday, as in post office and grocery store conversations. Fatherhood inevitably comes up in conversation as life wears on. "How are your children?" "What is X doing now?" "How was your trip to visit Y?" Archetypal pattern repeating itself if one can see it.

As I write this, I read in the newspaper the wrenching story of a nineteen-year-old master pole-vaulter from Penn State University, Kevin Dare, who crushed his skull and died in a vault similar to hundreds he'd done before. He went up normally, high but not outlandishly, then everything came apart. He let go of the pole, maybe thinking he was over the bar, and shot headfirst down and into the steel casing where he had placed the pole on the way up. What had happened? No one will know.[32]

Kevin's father, Ed Dare and his mother, Terri, were devastated. They witnessed the accident. Ed stood the entire eight hours of the visitation at a funeral home in State College at the

---

32 *New York Times*, February 28, 2002, section D, p. 5.

side of his son's casket. "I'll be here all day," he said, "next to my son." Kevin had said to him that morning in Minnesota, "This is my day, Dad."

That is fatherhood. That is mystery.

Passing Genes

The passing of genes is a natural archetypal propensity. Future is a religious notion. It finds its source in a mystery so deeply embedded in our psyche that we don't think of it as religion, so secular has our notion of religion become. Religion is now doctrine and organization to us, something on a census card.

What moves me here is that Ed Dare, who stood at the bier of his son, who could not leave the last he will ever see of his beloved, lost his genes forever. As his son dies, Ed is crushed, desperate, lost. His religion is built into him, quite aside from what stories or doctrine he might believe or thinks that he believes or what organization he belongs to.

What impacts that father's soul is not only the loss of his son's uniqueness but also the loss of his own future.

Phallos, understood as representing potency, is the *means* of a father's agency—his mode of becoming a biological father. Oh, it is too simple to put it only on phallos, only on erection, of course. The body and the psyche have too many intersecting systems to lay the entire meaning of masculinity only on one visible member, even metaphorically. I talk symbol here. Phallos is what men find and come to know as their gender talisman, the vehicle into which they pour intense meaning, that which they treasure as their identifying signification, their trademark, as it were, the means enabling their love, their essence, their substance. Phallos, if you will pardon the pun, stands for something.

Phallos is for a man what Jung called the Self, a notion even deeper in psyche than soul, that which rumbles about in his most private hidden moments, that to which he subjectively resorts when he lies abed in the quiet of the night, when he and it talk only to each other. This happens because phallos has a mind of its own, emanating from primal levels of the collective unconscious, a dimension quite distinct from ego.

Phallos is the means of a man's journey into the fog of the future, his own continuation beyond his own lifespan and into the blank sheet of a mysterious unknown. When Jung wrote of symbol, that may be close to what he meant. Without fatherhood, no father-future; all becomes mother.

Father as form/order

A child needs father as well as mother in ways beyond father's procreation. Classical Jungian thought holds that father brings a necessary order to join the organic plentitude of mother as an essential ingredient in children's development.

Without a present and functioning father in the family, a serious weakness results. The mother is a fabric of blood vessels, liquids, nurturing and accepting folds, mountains of milk, all essential, certainly, but not the whole story. Neither parent can provide everything that is needed in a family. Parents are archetypal opposites; they have need of one another if a whole kindred configuration is to take shape. Mother is round, as in breast and in womb. Father, being phallic, is vectored, since phallos is directed, long and narrow, aimed at something.

Children, encompassed in maternal circularity before birth, are assisted in adjusting to the outer world by a father's archetypal, linear presence, as in teaching a child worldly practicalities. In our day, with family disorganization being what it is, the father element is often provided only by institutions such as welfare agencies and schools, but while they are better than no outer structure at all, father absence leaves great gaps, since there is no intense personal connection to the child.

Another way of noting the importance of fatherhood is to consider the paradoxical qualities of pushing. Phallic mien is engrossed in push, just as the birthing mother pushes, but in quite a different way. Mother pushes out, father pushes in, and each is oppositionally related to the "in-ness" quality of mother, the "out-ness" quality of father. How to understand this paradox? As I speak of it here, each gender moves against its natural direction (father in, mother out) in conception and birth, an indication of the alchemical *opus contra naturam,* the paradoxical quality that characterizes all psychological development in the individual. Ergo, a man's fatherhood, which begins by his phallic in-pushing during coitus, thereafter demonstrates its potency through outer leadership, guiding his child to a connection with the world beyond the family. Yet, psychophysically, each parent functions paradoxically at the outset to enable conception, the start of new life, to take place. A male engages fatherhood by obeying his instinct and his mystic impulse, pushing in, and then, once the child is alive, his fatherhood provides wherewithal enabling the mother to protect what he has helped to bring into being. Then, as the years of childhood move on, he pushes the child out into the world. In both cases, the father must be aggressive. Rumi wrote:

> Your old grandmother says, "Maybe you shouldn't
> go to school. You look a little pale."
>
> Run when you hear that.
> A father's stern slaps are better.
>
> ...The severe father wants spiritual clarity.
> He ... leads you into the open.[33]

Paternal responsibility is not the same as the maternal one. He is stern, not sympathetic. The grandmother beckons the boy in. The father's slaps push the meek child beyond the comforts of the house. That is where the boy will find his fate. The child, particularly a son, needs his father's example and his teaching. The mother starts the push into the world. The father completes it.

Fatherhood responsibility as penetrator, as in push and intrusion, as worldly teacher for his child's encounters "out there,"

---

33 "The Core of Masculinity," in Rumi, *The Essential Rumi*, p. 115.

corresponds to his nature as a male and his role as a parent. The father prepares his son, especially, for the world. His *gnosis,* his knowledge of, for example, what it takes to win and keep a woman, or mayhap his courage to leave the family for pressing personal reasons, resonate throughout the family drama. No pleasure of enticing new dollies can substitute for such a rock-bottom establishment of potency, whether or not the mother and father continue to be physical lovers throughout their marriage. There are many intrusions—health, differing erotic propensities, the needs of work and community, variations of intellectual stimulation, life-style differences, dependencies, parental and grandparental interests—which sometimes do not become apparent until riper years. Yet the essential father functions do not seem to change. A man who is proud of his fatherly accomplishments finds great solace in them and they remain with him until the end.

A man who has gained his personal father *gnosis* from his experience as begetter, provider and teacher can see its roots in his own youth as a son, his early trial-and-error adolescence and his adult sacrifices, love and commitment. Liberated from the intense day-to-day nurturing of his mother, through his hard-earned oedipal freedom, a male comes into a new nature and experience of himself, coalescing into his ability to see and foresee the problems his children might have. He becomes a worried guide. This does not happen unless the father seizes the day and reflects. And, of course, one day he must stop worrying and let go, as must the mother—another stage in archetypal parenting.

Starbucks at Notting Hill Gate

Starbucks and fatherhood? If it is possible for pachysandra to suggest a way into mystical masculinity, then it is possible for a coffee shop to do so in its own way as well. Especially if the Starbucks is in our daughter's neighborhood and Barbara and I have just arrived in London for a three-month visit to reacquaint ourselves with the five of them: daughter-wife, husband and three grandchildren. There was a Starbucks just up the street from our house rental at Notting Hill Gate and I found it the day after we moved in.

Fatherhood prompts a man to do strange things, like, in my case, up and leaving Pennsylvania, a semi-retired practice, a house standing alone in the country, and an internet connection that I had doubts would ever work in London. Starbucks appeared when we were fresh off the plane. Many things didn't work right in our tiny house and the landlord did not answer his phone. What the hell am I doing here anyway, spending a small fortune, shivering in the bleak early April cloud and rain, twenty blocks from the kids, with legs that don't work right and with my mountain-hiker wife trundling on ahead, me feeling increasingly decrepit and lonely in her wake.

Starbucks, however one feels about its cultural influence, is as good a place as any—coffee drinker or not—to ponder serious things. And so, routinely, I did just that.

Fatherhood came upon me later than for most men. I knew, long before I came across Jung, that I would tread only a semi-conventional path in life, even if I had no name for what I was doing. Large parts of me were like other guys but odd things happened to me, like moving from the Presbyterian Church to the Episcopal Church and then to Anglo-Catholicism within that community, and then being ordained and spending five years as vicar in Bemidji in Minnesota's frozen north, where there were few eligible women. Like falling in love with a college girlfriend who ditched me in my first months in seminary. I wandered through ten years missing her and batting-out with several re-mote possibilities. There was a sense in me that I was meant to have a family but a man can't—or couldn't at that time—have children by himself. Thank the Lord that I did not panic and set-tle for less.

I look at the Starbuck's people, some just sitting and looking out, vacantly, maybe over a newspaper, especially men. Is that vacant gaze an inward one? Are their souls wandering as geysers of testosterone pound at their phallic door, puzzling about missing the boat by minutes? What if they had done this, done that? Would there be a special friend, an erotic friend, a romper room? Where is she now that she has sailed away? Are the guys staring out the window at Starbuck's like I remember myself being at twenty-five or thirty, holding a coffee, adrift in this lonely aspect of myself, hoping for more than a cup in my hand? Seminary had no answer for this. Nothing does. One is at the mercy of fate.

While in London, Barbara and I made our second trip to the Normandy Beaches, this time for the 60th anniversary of D-Day (see more below, in the chapter on spirit). On our first visit, several years before, in one of the museums near the landings, while casually watching at a long distance a film of troops going ashore, I saw a soldier jump from his landing craft as it ran up on the sand. He looked up and took a German bullet and fell into the sea. In articles about that day, the words often used to described what those men felt was "terrified," "bloody well frightened," "everybody scared to death."[34]

Where is fatherhood for those men in the water, those men's children, both born and unconceived? I think of that film image and those quotations and I am touched in my core. Their potency died with them, the potency of penetration and the potency of guidance for their children. Their fatherhood ended, perhaps before it began. I had my difficult ten-year wait until Barbara came along and made my fatherhood possible but that was as nothing compared to that man I saw fall at his disembarkation on D-Day. I grieve for those men, holding within myself a piece of their loss, a brotherhood with the dispossessed, another soul-marking. I realized, as I watched and even now as I write this several years later, and as I read Stephen Ambrose's book in preparation for our 2004 visit, that their loss is also my loss. Their fatherhood, real or potential, was forever ruined.

---

34 Stephen Ambrose, *D-Day*, p. 167.

Take-away fatherhood

Sitting in take-away Starbucks, I wonder about take-away (as the British call "take-out") fatherhood. Certainly many men marry women wrong for them and then beget children and then, as years wear on, come to know that wrongness and move away. It may be better for the commonweal that both men and women have the ability to do this, as compared to earlier times when one lived trapped forever by a choice no longer valid. But fatherhood has an archetypal quality of its own. A man may leave a family, but fatherhood cannot be left. A man's begetting with the "wrong" woman is, to a large extent, the fault of the man, the result of his stupidity, his panic, his projections, taking his pleasure without taking responsibility for knowing himself or the costs of that pleasure or the future of his seed. Fatherhood is of cosmic importance. No wonder we speak of God the Father.

It is not my point here to give marriage advice or to judge any man's actions, which can be done only by a man on the basis of what his soul requires. Rather, it is to call men's attention to their need for wakefulness, or, as the Buddhists and Quakers would say, mindfulness, as they celebrate their sexuality. Because fatherhood is a primal and inherently phallic attribute, one cannot dismiss the conception of a new human being as being of less importance than a man's personal happiness or gratification, important as these are. Men must be mindful of whom they impregnate, which is why we have marriage traditions and family laws, a linear concern established to protect paternity, among other things. Traditions and laws serve to preserve hard-fought-for civilization, to preserve order and security. To abrogate law and tradition requires strong justification. We are not to step aside from either without a spiritually overriding necessity.

Frank Conroy wrote:

> Perhaps love between father and child starts in mutual curiosity, but wherever it comes from, it quickly grows, if all goes well, to *a force as powerful as anything a man will ever experience.* A true solace

against loneliness, against the tyranny and emergency of self.[35]

A Jungian might well translate "self" in Conroy's remarks as "ego," but be that as it may, "a force as powerful as anything a man will ever experience" strikes me as worth noting, especially in the context of potency, fatherhood and soul. Conroy's "curiosity" on the part of the father certainly has to do with the wonder wrought by his probably instinct-driven physical penetration and tiny spurt, that darling little one grinning through his or her burgeoning brain connections, developing week by week. And blissfully smiling, as all that incredible brain work goes on unconsciously. The kid is a miracle; nature is a miracle and no natural miracle is as great as the creation and development of new life.

To casually or carelessly walk away from a work so auspiciously begun can be nothing short of criminal. Of course, if the soul demands it, that is not casual or careless but quite another matter and another writing.

The absolutely fierce need to procreate

Procreation means to move the creative process toward new life. Humans ordinarily think of creation as the province of God, of a force far greater than ego intention. Procreation means that human beings also have a role in creation—no, role is too facile a word. It's like saying that Barbra Streisand has a role in *Funny Girl*. Barbra Streisand *is* "Funny Girl"–with thanks, of course, to Fanny Brice and many others who made that remarkable play and film. Procreation is a good word because it does not displace a sense of the Creator. But collaboration between God and man—urperson—is the point here, as it is the point in soul. Man does not create. Man participates in archetypal creation as he himself has come into being and continues in his being by virtue of a power larger than his ego. His fatherhood is that important.

Our human need to procreate is fierce, as fierce as Sharon Olds

---

35 Sven Birkerts, book review of Frank Conroy, *Dogs Bark, But the Caravan Rolls on: Observations Then and Now,"* in *New York Times*, June 23, 2002 (italics added).

portrays in her poem "Greed and Aggression":

> Someone in Quaker meeting talks about greed and
>   aggression
> and I think of the way I lay the massive
> weight of my body down on you
> like a tiger lying down in gluttony and pleasure on the
> elegant heavy body of the eland it eats,
> the spiral horn pointing to the sky like heaven.
> Ecstasy has been given to the tiger,
> forced into its nature the way the
> forcemeat is cranked down the throat of the held goose,
> it cannot help it, hunger and the glory of
> eating packed at the center of each
> tiger cell, for the life of the tiger and the
> making of new tigers so there will
> always be tigers on the earth, their stripes like
> stripes of night and stripes of fire-light—
> so if they had a God it would be striped,
> burnt-gold and black, the way if
> I had a God it would renew itself the
> way you live and live while I take you as if
> consuming you, it would be a God of
> love as complete satiety,
> greed and fullness, aggression and fullness, the
> way we once drank at the body of an animal
> until we were so happy we could only
> faint, our mouths running, into sleep.[36]

The human need to survive and procreate is as intense as Olds portrays. Death can show this clearly, as I mentioned earlier in the story of the pole-vaulting son. I recall my emotional connection with my brother and sister-in-law when they lost their first-born, hit by a car when he was thirteen. I came from Zürich for the funeral and went with them when they first saw their son in his casket at a funeral home. I have never, before or since,

---

36 Robert Bly, James Hillman, Michael Meade, eds., *The Rag and Bone Shop of the Heart*, p. 327.

been so laid waste, being the only one present when faint with grief they first saw Robbie, saw the loss of his and their future. Dramatic everyday life, to be sure, experienced by everyday people, to be sure, but it sometimes slips by us that what goes on in everyday life is the instinct and archetype that we read and think about only as theory.

In 1992 with my daughter Kate, now the mother of the three children who drew us to London, I walked down the aisle of a stately church in the company of a crowd of friends and family to present her to her husband to be joined together by church and state. I love my daughter and I wanted her to have James as her mate and even then I loved James and wanted him to have Kate. I was quite proud—the wedding was a symbolic representation of what Barbara's and my life was about—escorting that lovely woman and giving our blessing to her and James's future life.

And when I look at our son Stephen, two years Kate's senior, and see him brawny as I have never been, and hear him, beautifully-toned introvert as I am only now struggling to be, socially-activist lawyer that he is, that I might have been but never was, great ladies' man, a fate that escaped me, now the fiancé of a lovely and intelligent woman, and see in him the outlines of my face, as I do also in my daughter, I am stunned with wonder at the outcome of my two effectual and aggressive outpourings, moving on in their own ways, over some forty-four years.

And as I look at father-creativity as it has visited me, the bottom line of mystery may be what Jung has called, I suspect in a rash and poetic moment, "absolute knowledge."[37] That sounds almost bizarre before one realizes that Jung writes of knowledge as *gnosis,* soul knowledge as seen from an introverted and subjective and mystical perspective. To be "absolute" means, to me, that "absolute knowledge" has no qualifying conditions. Knowl-

---

37 See, for instance, "Synchronicity: An Acausal Connecting Principle," *The Structure and Dynamics of the Psyche,* CW 8, pars.931, 948, and "Flying Saucers: A Modern Myth," *Civilization in Transition,* CW 10, pars. 636f.

edge that is absolute is not open to fundamental change nor is it mediated by fashion or conventional or laboratory data or by temporary disturbances. Creation belongs to the milieu of the world as having, in itself, the character of God, as the French Jesuit priest Teilhard de Chardin wrote.

Creation, as in fatherhood, as I use the term, comes into one's awareness as the product of a mystical perception, as in "forced into its nature . . . packed at the center of each tiger [human] cell," as Olds put it, as soul markings, as I have said above. My body "knows," even if my ego does not, what must be done to create, as any animal's does, a sign of God's presence, keeping life in the world. My body—and my soul—reveals itself by what it strains to do. That revelation moves me and me-in-the-world forward toward creative accomplishment. Once I am engaged in intercourse, nearing orgasm, there is little I can do to modify its outcome. Over the years, I am left to stand in awe and won- der—all of that, including those lovely grandchildren, as having come through *me*? Yes.

3
The Union of Opposites

Rejoining

The union of opposites has a classically archetypal structure, as we see clearly in Jung's vast writings on alchemy. What is joined together by natural gestation, like the child and the womb, must be broken apart, separated, for psychological growth to occur in either the mother or the child, a basic supposition in all depth psychology. What is thus broken by the wisdom, the "absolute knowledge," of nature in birth, and by subsequent individual development in childhood and thereafter, cries out, as life goes on, for a symbolic restoration of that lost condition of symbiosis. Union, reunion, presupposes separation, the *sine qua non* of consciousness, without which everyone remains caught in the innocence of childhood.

Childhood has a beauty and is, in families, dear, but it is dear only in the innocence of the young. If one looks at the rigors of instinctual life through the eyes of Sharon Olds, childhood does take one very far. Both the joy and anguish of (re)union still lie ahead.

Joining, or rejoining, looked at from the perspective of Jung, is led by the individuation process, the apex of personal, and, by extension, collective human development. Here is where Jung is, in spite of himself, Christian, since the individual person is primary. The individual points a way toward restoration for society; only when the individual moves toward restoration, and influences other persons to do so, can society transform. A man must return to his primal psychic elements, the archetypal mother, without being "caught" in the mother—what this means is not the point of this work—and he does so, or fails to do so, in his relationships with women, or his avoidance of them, in his

97

intimate relationships, his nurturance of friendships, in his nourishment of others, and in his death. Those are the ways psychological joining takes place in ordinary time.

The way I dwell on in this work is sexual union between opposites, as when ordinary human beings are pressed to join through intercourse. Since the opposites are essentially and commonly understood as male and female, they join in an archetypal configuration, a restorative pattern, dictated by hormonal and body form, that opens a way to the once-lost connection that the soul requires. The soul, being that invisible but clearly experienced core of individual life, seen subjectively and in depth, does not exist in isolation. It requires relationship and community. Community, seen in personal terms, finds its zenith in the union of two bodies and two souls, which is perhaps better seen as a reunion, a recapitulation of urperson, a way, if not *the* way, that primal separation has at least the theoretical possibility of being overcome. Thus the union of opposites is the spiritual goal of physical sexual union as that union accomplishes its promise as the paradigm of reconciliation. In the sexual union of opposites—male and female—the visible and the invisible find a way to reflect one another and declare their symbiosis.

Paradox yet again

Such is the unrelenting path to redemption in religious language, to wholeness in psychological language. The course of this reunion is profoundly paradoxical: what we do not want, we need, as in the sharing demanded by love. What we need we avoid, as in a love connection that has the potential of returning us to a state of wholeness. Paradox is at the core of the mystery. What a man must have, after the complexities of the fierce labor of establishing his masculine identity as a genuine and separate individual, as an inner sense of himself as male, is a re-union with the mother psychic element, the feminine. If this is to work, it must be at a far distance from his own mother (since incest is altogether dangerous and forbidden) with but a faint glow of the

mother-son lost identification. A man's separate way is apart
from his mother, for there is no genuine phallic maleness if he is
in her pocket, yet the archetypal mother, paradoxically as well,
must be part of his psychological undergirding. The route is his
penetration, his parallel entering again "her pocket," the ritual
path called for in the union of opposites, noted by the Church,
in marriage, as a parallel to the union of Christ and the Church.
As a man moves into his female partner, he mystically returns
to the place of his origin, the place of metapsychological beginnings. The suggestion of unisex hovers over the actions of intercourse.

The female as mystery food for a male

A man's turning from patriarchal dominance to erotic surrender,
from entitlement to human equality, and his finding a new kind
of power in his need, finds its apogee in sexual intercourse. A
man enters strongly and forcefully, explodes, then, limp and
spent, withdraws. This paradox, strong leading to weak, and
weak—as surrender—becoming strong, can be misinterpreted by
the man as a loss, even an evil, the fault of his male-female connection and a reason for anger, resentment and avoidance. His
being spent as a man after intercourse is itself an aspect of paradox, for in his subsequent weakness a man will find in himself an
explication of his wholeness as a human being, of his participation in life's basic rhythm, which he finds is part of his own participation and not the sole possession of women, a powerful reason for his abandonment of patriarchy.

If a man cannot grasp what is happening to him, he can react
self-righteously, either in the event or after hundreds of events.
For what happens in sexual union is a paradigm of the meaning
of life itself. A man must come to know that he is a partner, the
leader in the dance, perhaps, if his leadership inspires his partner
to follow, but never a dictator, as his post-coital impotence
demonstrates. It is necessary for him to be strong, but after sex
is not the time. His leadership goes nowhere without the coop-

eration of his dance partner. He needs her and is dependent upon her even as he leads. His acknowledgment of his weakness is his strength. He descends into her warmth after his own strength is spent.

Desire built upon attraction is a sign to which all males pay attention. Desire comes from the depths of a male's being, from his incompleteness as a total person which his soul whispers in his psychic ear, his hunger for a restored wholeness. Phallos is his divining rod, demanding his attention as in Jung's "absolute knowledge." If this does not happen for a male, something has crippled him. Eros is a god in the unconscious and must be obeyed.

If a man is more or less comfortable in his skin as a man, that is to say, if he feels himself a gender apart and separate from the feminine, a justifiable member of half the human race, well-connected with phallic instinct as it works in him, he is half way on track, not the whole way. He must know his hunger and he must know the food that will satisfy. In falling in love with a woman, a man feels that she is what he has been seeking, that she causes the veil to fall from his eyes, that she is his banquet of delight, that she is his lost other half. In the sexual expression of his desire, he delights in finding himself. But the plot thickens. Even without a heart-felt love, in a man's penetration of a woman he finds a restorative power coming into his subjective awareness, something that smells like, tastes like, completeness. He discovers in his need, his itch, his craving, an intensity that tells him who he is and what he needs to do. In intercourse he approaches the center of his mystery.

The sensation of intercourse is a revelation; friction and in-tensity build excitement into a crescendo of anticipation. It may occur to him that he himself is doing this, that his penis, even his life, was made for this, that his body is in a kind of cosmic escalation. He finds himself playing out his masculine destiny in a huge and subjective burst of rapture. He is into a woman, touching the most personal and guarded parts of her, pressing his phallic reality upon her, meeting her receptive nature as wanting him to be doing what he is doing. As his phallos becomes part of her, her vagina becomes part of him. This is nothing less than architectonic. The opposites become union in the act of making love, which scripture says is the definition of God. A man is established as a male, what every man needs since his separation from his birth source and the grief of his oedipal struggle. He establishes himself in union with his symbolic mother surrogate; he is restored to original belonging. That is why making love for a man is the magical adventure that it is.

What of woman does a man need? The soft cocoon of her opening to him provides him with a home. Even when a man is not sure of love from a woman, he knows of his potential inherent in his need of penetration, his need to experience the power of the archetypal presence he carries and which she wants. That is how he is designed. Because he is phallic, he cannot avoid his need to penetrate, feeding on love, on her gentleness, whether or not she is gentle. His genes require it and his phallos requires it. Welcome or not, in love or not, he has little choice but to follow his design. Such a design, of course, produces all sorts of trouble, since his opposite is genuinely an individual person as well as an opposite and not simply a vessel for his requirements. But ah, the delicious food for his soul a loving woman provides. The core press for their union, from the masculine side, is always the subjective, inner demand for genetic, or, as Jungians would say, archetypal expression. Were it not for the magnetic draw of the feminine promise of union, it might be that a man could happily spend his life watching himself in his bathroom mirror.

The Goat or Who is Sylvia

Barbara and I saw *The Goat* by Edward Albee during our three-month stay in London, beautifully acted by Jonathan Pryce and directed by Anthony Page. The play is chock full of opposites: Martin (Pryce) and Stevie, his wife; Martin, a straight man and Billy, his gay son; Martin, the secret lover of Sylvia, the goat;

and Martin, a man hiding his profound, if strange, love, and Ross, his once-trusted friend who betrays him to his wife. The subtitle of the play, "Who is Sylvia?" is the question posed for the audience. Sylvia, the goat, is revealed early on as Martin's partner in an affair, so that is not the question. The question is the meaning of Sylvia for Martin, who expresses a quite beautifully and amazing sense of other-worldly passion and respect for his animal lover.

Goats, as we know, are lecherous animals who endlessly attempt to multiply, as do rabbits. Martin expresses real spiritual heights when he tells Ross, and especially Stevie, something of the full length and depth of his passion. One can excuse Ross, who is a bit of a clod, for not understanding any of what Martin tries to tell him but Stevie, his wife, and Billy, his son, are the real problems. Here is a woman who has been married to a man for years, has shared his bed and board, has made all of the proper marriage noises and moves but when her man is exposed as dealing with an inner problem, she can only be personally hurt and rather brutally brittle in her expression of that hurt. Not a suggestion of sympathy or understanding or desire to understand proceeds from her, not even an honest curiosity about what in the world could be going on with her husband. She can only express anger. Here is a real problem with the opposites. Selfishness intrudes.

Stevie does not mourn what she sees as Martin's departure for another. She is resentful, destructive. In her eyes, she has been abandoned, replaced. Martin is engaged with something he himself cannot quite fathom. As they are taken by each other, goat Sylvia looks at Martin with wonderment in her eyes. Apparently Martin sees Sylvia as his means of connection to a genuine "other," something totally beyond his expectations and deeper than he has as yet found in his life, including with his wife.

I suspect that Billy, the son, is a recrudescence of Albee's own gay story. It was the talk of London that Billy kisses his father erotically when he sees that his father is really in love and in some ways even as queer as he. Yet the issue in the play is not who one loves but whether one experiences love as a divine presence quite aside from how it is publicly denominated, whether the union of opposites can be seen as an important, even structural, occasion in society, worthy of curiosity, regardless of the object of that love. That Albee has the insight and creative skill to write so powerfully and to question conventionality in so radical a form as he does in the play demonstrates his importance in modern theater. As he himself states in an interview printed in the London theater program, "The play is about love, loss, the limits of tolerance and who, indeed, we really are."

With regard to who we really are, I deal here only with Martin's subjective, quite mystical, and quite physical (for that aspect of his infatuation is what makes the play grist for my mill) quite "oppositional" affair with goat Sylvia. Martin acquiesces in his obedience to an urgent inner demand to bridge his and Sylvia's genetic difference, using love and phallic potency as the bridge. Martin seems to know, and believe in, in a frightened, awestruck way, the transcendent quality of what has happened to him, catching him totally by surprise and spreading confusion into the way he lives and the people he lives with. Martin is quite believable as an ordinary genuine man, enmeshed in quite an ordinary marriage to Stevie, whom he seems to genuinely want to protect and respect. He is a dumbfounded man, caught up in an inexplicable quandary, as any man is who finds himself bound up with a mystical experience that goes against the social grain or inner precept. The profundity of his love for Sylvia and what has happened to him in the midst of it goes against his grain, as a man who, up to the entry of Sylvia into his life, has been content with the ordinary. But he has another urge, different from the social.

The amazing thing about Martin's devotion to Sylvia, or, better said, his experience of the depth of their union, is his unremitting loyalty to his personal experience. He knows what has happened to him and he stands by it in spite of the fierce accusations of his wife, his friend and, up to a point, his son.

Men (and women too) can learn from Martin's honesty and openness, letting the consequences of a strange affliction be what they may, choosing to honor one's experience rather than continue to hide it. The impression it left with me was powerfully mystical. His halting attempts to "explain" to Stevie went nowhere—how could they not? Martin's love for Sylvia went way beyond Stevie's ken. She is offended to her core (or lack of core). She throws prized pottery about, slashes paintings in her rage. She is angry beyond words, but words she has aplenty. Revenge coagulates in her mind. Martin perceives a foretaste of disintegration in his.

Albee's treatment of one bizarre union of opposites (the denouement must be held back here) displays wild imagination. Wild imagination is called for. The play is about the psychological collapse of normal expectations, about the fantastic that lurks around the Dionysian corner of mystery, about a love— beyond what we know—that truly dare not speak its name. That is what a man might come up with were he to reflect upon, let his imagination wander among, the more bizarre urgings of eros. Such peculiarities come to us in dreams, which the terrified ego has little power to censor. Dreams come and suggest things because they wait in the unconscious. The union of opposites is not child's play.

One flesh

When bodily sensation and soul urging give him his clue, a man seeks a welcoming place where phallos might rise up and lay its seed as though it were an animal obedient to instinct, making some little sense of Sylvia. A man is filled with wonder as he anticipates his desired reception and the female's delight in his presence within her and the wonders it might provoke. His astonishment is his being wanted, not feared as a reckless invader or put aside by pietistic or parental obedience. The ground is thus laid for a fulfillment of mystical portent, the healing of long-suffered, anguished separation, as in the *parousia*, the second coming of Christ.

The female body is abstruse and foreign to a man, vastly different from his own. Can he know that body, can he enter and imaginatively possess it for a moment, can he come to know an opposite person and find joy there for a moment, can he be transformed so that his and his lover's difference becomes minimal, even passes away as an obstacle—thus imaginatively reconnecting with urperson? That, I think, is the meaning be-' hind the Christian teaching that in marriage—indeed, I would say in any sexual union—the two become "one flesh," and the now sadly abandoned vow taken at the presentation of the wedding rings, "with my body I thee worship."[38] The idea is, of course, their sexual union, extended into a life communion. The sexual bridging of the gender opposites in marriage is seen by the Church to approximate the original unity that mythologically existed before the opposites split apart. The physical intercourse —union—of male and female is a harbinger of the rapturous end of separation. Whether a man consciously or unconsciously realizes the symbolism of his sexual act, he does so nonetheless; he participates in union and that symbolism even if unconsciously, physically entering the metapsychology of his being as he lustily pants in his bed and zigzags in his mind.

I have a Jungian colleague who claims that every man unconsciously wants to be a woman, and that that is the secret motivation behind phallic penetration/aggression. This, maybe, comes close to what he means. The union of opposites is a complex notion, as any observation of coupling demonstrates, but it casts a serious light on a human behavior that in present-day culture has become, often, so perfunctory that it approaches banality.

As seen though a phallic lens, the means to beget connects union with creation. A man's inner deprivation, his lack of womb, provides goal and direction to phallos. If he is excited,

---

38 Church of England Book of Common Prayer, pp. 304, 314.

that is, if he is erect, his male hormonal foundation calls for expression and he hears the call of his masculinity as a psychic demand for obedience. Invisible spirit, working through body, tips him off. If he gets it, he plunges on in sweaty sex on his way to climax. That is the point, at this juncture, of potency as the expression of a man's genetic and archetypal destiny.

The union of opposites is an alchemical and archetypal configuration of original wholeness reconstituted as a biological/psychological goal, an ordinarily unconscious image standing behind the human impulse aiming at completion. No man can healthfully live in isolation and loneliness and he will find a solution to his emptiness, whether it be sexual union or some spiritual variation of reunion. Every man feels that he needs another, an "object" in his life and usually that other is an opposite. Mythologically, one might look at the ancient tale Plato told of the original urperson, what we have innocently called anthropos, which divided into two sexes what was originally a unity, which mankind has forever after sought a way to reunite.

It would be quite remarkable for a man about to engage in sex to imagine that in doing so he will participate in a mythological/cosmological restoration. Few do, of course, but nearly every man knows that something extraordinarily important is happening even though he would be hard pressed to give it a name. Some men feel that sex is holy but do not pursue the matter.

For a man to begin to unravel the "importance" of his phallic nature requires his moving to a deeper level of understanding in his psyche, his nurturing of his fantasy life, his pressing himself to grasp something he can only understand by following the leadership of his body. A man does not have to think—thinking can ruin sexual pleasure—but he does need to wonder. In coming together with an opposite, a man is subjectively connecting with a mythological galaxy of foreignness, accounting for the stars in his eyes. He is accomplishing "one flesh," both a literal event via intercourse and a symbolic reality reaching down into the mists of the unconscious. In making love, a new world comes into being, as well as possibly a new life. For a man to perceive the power inherent in his providing a phallic bridge for the union of opposites, his imagination must come into play as a counterpart to his sexual playing. As he feels his lack of and need for the feminine, his requirement for completion, a man can discover a sense of his metapsychological condition and destiny, not as much through understanding as through his emotional need. Union fills in "feeling" blanks in evolution and heredity in a man's *gnosis*. A man's sense of deprivation due to primal gender split prompts his phallic urge toward remedy.

Human biology begs certain questions that human psyche and curiosity strain to answer. What might be the purpose for sexual intercourse having the form that it does? Certainly it is not the only way evolution might have moved. And why insemination in and of itself? Why the huge sensitivity of the male sexual organs? Why the sexual opposites, for that matter? Aside from the technical genetic reasons, after-the-fact explorations of the way things work, let us suppose that psyche itself came into being to bring separated phenomena together to facilitate new life, the root product of the union of opposites. Required in that process is the factor of "doing," of instigation, of agent of change, inducer of union, of a male's badly wanting sex and, of course, of penetration. Change happens when opposites flirt with one another and come together, with the extravagant physical occurrences of romance providing the impetus. Males are half of the human opposition and males find themselves with the physical and psychological equipment that aim to express union and to fertilize. Intercourse is the dispositional form of the union. A male entering into congress seeks not only relief from both ontological and existential isolation, but also an acting role in cooperation with the metabolism of the universe. That is known as the transpersonal aspect of psychology.

For a man to live without an opposite is to languish without that role to play. He can find substitutes and sublimations, of course, but in them he must still metaphorically live out his phallic nature. To live with an opposite involves living in anguish if the two cannot find a way to fit together; not mesh but fit. Even if they fit, in some poetic way, they will not always coincide. A man must continually woo his opposite, for that is his masculine fate—to assist her wanting to fit with him, to know that a major part of his male role is to seduce in a way that embellishes his woman. His self-reflection is meant to bring him to that understanding. He can never successfully force or pressure her accommodation, and to imagine that he can is the basic patriarchal error. The female draws the male in and to do so she must desire him. She is to be as honey to the phallos and the man so that he will put his stinger out.

It is easy to oversimplify relationship in union. Union requires that each partner not only give to and receive from one another but that their souls as well as their bodies find a way to fit and join to make the alchemy work. For a man, this means that, say, when he looks into his partner's eyes, he sees something in those eyes that he must have.

A man who in his younger years kept company with prostitutes never looked into their eyes, even avoided connecting with their faces. He was interested only in managing his own erotic needs; the woman was only his way to do so, his means of masturbation, so to speak. A major requirement for that man in therapy was to find a way to know that he also carried the feminine within himself—that by avoiding eye-soul-expression with his partner he was avoiding an urgently important aspect of himself. He was cheating his lover. He was cheating himself.

Coniunctio oppositorum

This classical alchemical trinity then produces the relationship of male to female as *the supreme and essential opposition*. . . . This [totality] is produced only by the synthesis of male and female. . . . the final synthesis of male and female is an achievement of the art and a product of conscious endeavor. The result of the synthesis was consequently conceived by the adept [the novice, seeker, learner]as self-knowledge, which, like the knowledge of God, is needed for the preparation of the Philosophers' Stone.[39] Piety is needed for the work, and this is nothing but the knowledge of oneself.[40]

The emphasis on "self-knowledge" in the above passage certainly resonates for me when I recall my struggle to articulate the first chapter of this book, "Mystical Aspects of Masculine Sexuality." Jung's modern discovery of alchemy as a paradigm for psychological development is unparalleled and unexcelled in contemporary thought. The reader who is intrigued or even unsettled by Jung's use of alchemical imagery is encouraged to delve into the matter. The resources for such a delving are readily available in his writings and in subsequent commentaries by others.[41] Let it be said, at this juncture, that such an idea as the union of opposites, and my using it as a means of understanding the masculine side of that union, could not have been done without Jung's massive commitment to alchemical symbolism.

Coniunctio oppositorum is alchemical language for the union of opposites. *Coniunctio* confounds the rational mind. It is commonly assumed that unlike elements cannot be united. Yet there is union in every family we encounter, in every couple we know, in every surprising collaboration of disparate factors we meet. *Coniunctio* is not at all unusual; it meets us at every hand in everyday life. Seeing *coniunctio* everywhere is a sign that a mystical consciousness is growing in us and that patriarchy is beginning to breathe its last. *Coniunctio* is a mental concept that enables us to articulate how it might be that modest pachysandra and her delightful rain-dance or a boy who loves the moon both send a gentle message about the nature of the universe and how it

---

39 The Philosophers' Stone, for the alchemists, refers to the end product of the work, the *lapis lazuli*, what the Bible calls "the pearl of great price." For Jung, it is the great, soulful, probably unattainable yet final human psychological accomlishment, approximated in individuation.

40 *Mysterium Coniunctionis*, CW 14, pars. 656f. (italics added).

41 See especially Edward F. Edinger, *The Mysterium Lectures, The Aion Lectures,* and *The Mystery of the Coniunctio.*

is revealed.

Jung wrote that "the kind of effect it [whatever one is con-templating, even, presumably, pachysandra, the moon or one's erection] will have depends to a large extent on the attitude of the conscious mind." Attitude has heretofore been discussed. At-titude "implies that what is called for is the renewal of an ego position."[42] Emphasis: renewal. A man's ego position—how he says he values his union—may contradict how he behaves, which leaves a lover/spouse in an untenable place. A man might not be aware of how his attitude contradicts his statements. But *con-iunctio's* requirement of authenticity cannot be gainsaid. *Con-iunctio* cannot be pretended any more than erection can be pre-tended. One's partner in union can sniff it out and within herself she knows. It stands at the core of the union.

The struggle for communion

Human life is rent and torn by opposition, animosities, struggles for power. The need for cooperation has perhaps never been greater; nuclear proliferation, terrorism and unilateral war-making make us all feel unsafe, vulnerable, morally decimated. What happens among groups of people also happens between individuals and particularly between men and women, whose needs for union push them together and whose ambitions, authority hungers and ego needs drive them apart. For they, as Jung wrote, are "the supreme and essential opposition," a for-mula set for both grace and disaster.

It behooves us, then, as we examine potency by way of under-standing masculinity, to continue to examine the masculine side of Jung's "supreme and essential opposition," the split in gender that is the *mise en scène* of union. The alchemists' notion, bor-rowed by Jung, is that the supreme manifestation of human op-posites lies in our gender differences, mirrored in the Biblical im-agery of the Fall. The alchemists' solution is found in the *con-*

---

42 Samuels et al, *A Critical Dictionary*, p. 35.

iunctio, the coitus of the king and queen in the bath, much like the oriental notion of the yin and the yang moving in the same direction, each partaking of the other, producing new life. The begetting of new life through the union of male and female opposites always has a mystical base and is routinely portrayed in ancient mythology as something close to a miracle. Everyday, anyone who has watched an infant develop into a beginning person and then become an adult can understand the sense of awe that comes upon a parent or any observant person.

Stimulating a male's urgent desire to unite with a female is an enormous metapsychological pressure for reunion, which *coniunctio,* the possibility of which underlies his phallic nature, imposes upon him. He is not himself, quite, when under the sway of testosterone. His ego bends to its demands. Hardly ever is a man conscious of the drawing power of the *coniunctio,* so deeply is it embedded in the unconscious. It silently angles his erotic behavior toward the feminine as a natural course of events after puberty. (That it does not clearly do so in homosexual males and some others, or does so in symbolic but not physical ways, is a question worthy of pursuit but which cannot be dealt with in this work.) A male experiences his erotic restlessness both as pleasure and as suffering. A man cannot help but live through the pain of passion, for his part in the restoration of wholeness is hard labor, requiring the continual sacrifice of his childish love of ease. He plays his phallic part in the transcendent mysteries of restitution and joins the work of God in creation. So doing, he becomes God's agent, which if all were known, every man seeks to be.

A man would not be who he is without such a challenge. It is a responsibility entailing great honor. That which drives a man to engage in so bridging with a metaphysical and metapsychological opposite is his personal response to the primal separation of the sexes. It requires, as Jung said, a "knowledge of oneself" and, as well, an obedience to oneself, a commitment to honor his personal experience of eros.

A man must first accept himself as a man, inherently different and separate from his female partner, something that requires heroic stamina in his early developmental stages. As an adult male, he finds himself a foreigner to the feminine. He is enormously curious about her as "other territory," as my London Jungian colleague Diana Grace-Jones has called it. When a man is enthralled, it is as though he were an explorer in foreign and exotic parts, making maps where none existed, at least for him. He plunges through the undergrowth, follows his newly discovered route and is led by a gleam. Beyond enthrallment, the difficulties as well as the pleasures are tantalizing and endless. One can understand the alchemists' placement of the *opus,* the work, in a laboratory.

The two are brought together through sexual attraction, since sexuality brings into focus both devotion and commitment, without which sexuality can become a recurring narcissistic fantasy. Since the phallos is obvious and penetrates, masculinity is, as already said, the commonly considered "active" agent in union, often interpreted as the "dominant" agent (opening the door to patriarchy), which may give the impression that the authentic feminine never instigates or dominates, and is simply receptive. But in fact the feminine begets connection as much as the masculine; she beguiles, flirts, entices, entrances. She invites penetration; that is part of her mystery for a man.

I used to sit on a street bench in the Notting Hill Gate neighborhood, sometimes for half an hour. I could hear the approach of an enticing woman by the sound of her heels—click, click, click—on the stone of the sidewalk, like a mating call. That is nothing if not active. Not every woman has shoes that make that sound. I watched their faces. Many were aware that I was watching. Those are the sanctus bells of union.

There are ways of gentle and careful penetration by males. But even rough sex, which is fancied by some women, has a certain profundity embedded within it, just as the unrelenting and harsh Hound of Heaven does. It seems likely to me that phallos enables feminine authority by impregnating and then turning

matters over to her. The union of opposites poses many intriguing questions while suggesting a secret solution which men
and women are continually striving to grasp.

The *coniunctio* secret

The secret embedded in *coniunctio* is the way in which everyday
human life moves toward a resolution through embedded human
needs. Jungians would say that such needs are archetypal, ger-
mane to the great mystery. Philosophers call this teleology, the
study of the "end" or ultimate purpose entrenched in natural
processes. The secret is religious in that it points to a transcendent meaning. It is not religious in a doctrinal or ecclesiastical
sense; rather it is religious in a psychological sense: gnostic
rather than clerical. It deals with psyche's hidden intention as
the background of behavior and raises questions about the *telos,*
the purpose of life. People might find a solution in a traditional
religious container, or a partial solution, as I do to an extent, but
one need not do so. The important factors are one's spiritual
attitude, one's ego modesty and one's subjective awareness.

The union of opposites is a concept useful to masculine definition because it suggests that male potency has purpose, psychological importance and intensity. Bodily penetration is one's
first thought regarding male participation, understandably. Important and suggestive as that notion is, it leads to a wider application. Phallic experience extends its reach metaphorically into
areas and boundaries that are not physical, but soulful, mental
and spiritual. Union contributes to what Jungian psychology always strives to express: a sense of mystery and meaning to ordinary human events, not only illness and pathology but also am-
bition and accomplishment. As well as acknowledging the frailty
of separation, union acknowledges the reality of the unconscious
human press for reunion. The secret is the mend, the final result,
that all human beings intend in whatever faulty or effective ways
they may function. That is communion.

It occurs to me, as I write this, that the 2004 celebration of the fiftieth anniversary of the American Supreme Court decision in Brown v. Board of Education, outlawing "separate but equal" racial education calls to mind a collective, social aspect of the union of opposites, however inadequately that decision has been put into practice. Genuine suffering pushed that decision into American history, and blacks and whites, seeking full implementation, even now do so with an unrelenting passion to overcome discriminatory boundaries. That restless need is psychologically attuned to union and to my mind is lovingly erotic and religious.

The union of opposites as an overarching metapsychological goal of phallic intensity, and penetration is a notion that puts one close to the spirit element of my work, yet to come. Let it only be said, at this point, that a man's intense interest in sexual union is bound up with his identity as a man, his insertive, aggressive and intruding nature, his interior as well as his outward bodily calling. Union brings to notice male instinctual need and complements the human need to be whole.

Urperson—androgyne

Jung paraphrases the Midrash Rabbah VIII, in the Jewish mystical tradition, as saying,

> He (Adam) is an androgyne, or a man and woman grown into one body with two faces. God sawed the body in two and made each half a back. Through his androgyny Adam has affinities with Plato's sphere-shaped Original Being.[43]

The mythology of the separated androgyne, or urperson, stands as a backdrop to a consideration of the union of opposites, as stated earlier. Playing a mind game with oneself, one can see the Midrash story and the Platonic paradigm as providing us now with a mythological sense of how it was that males and females were once a united entity which then became separated, leaving it to us, following heart and instinct, to find a way back

---

43 *Mysterium Coniunctionis*, CW 14, par. 587.

to an approximation of an original equality of being, androgyny, urperson or wholeness. The inner pressure for a union of opposites is a hallmark of that need. Each of the sexes is physically made for such a union. One has an insertion organ, the other has a receptive organ, with each being desired by the other and likely to be fascinated by it. Out of their erotic need something new has the opportunity to emerge. Each of the sexes finds a compelling impetus toward— or aversion to (but, again, that is another story)—its opposite, giving each a symbolic semblance of fateful completion. A man reaches, or pushes, out. It is phallos, or its equivalent as tongue, finger or attitude, establishing that reach. But phallos is the image of the extension that reaches.

A man need not depend upon alchemy, to say nothing of Jung, to move beyond patriarchy. One finds the root of union in early and childish invention the young apply to what they perceive, for the miracle of love and new birth cries out for explanation and incites imagination. Adults, never lacking that interest, find it in fiction, observation, pornography and gossip, in mythology and ancient story. Metaphorical extensions of the union of opposites—in personal experience, politics, art, committee work and neighborly relationships—find expression in human beings the world over.

Union is archetypal. Its metaphorical equivalences are everywhere.

4
Ecstasy

The Fountains mingle with the River,
And the Rivers with the Ocean,
The winds of Heaven mix for ever
With a sweet emotion;
Nothing in the world is single;
All things by a law divine
In one spirit meet and mingle.
Why not I with thine?—

See the mountains kiss high Heaven
And the waves clasp one another;
No sister-flower would be forgiven
If it disdained its brother,
And the sunlight clasps the earth
And the moonbeams kiss the sea:
What is all this sweet work worth
If thou kiss not me?[44]

Threshold/heroic action

That which propels a man into establishing himself sexually is the uniquely male experience of orgasm, which, once it happens, never wears out its welcome. Some men want orgasm only with a loved person, with whom a broad kind of sharing can take place. Others will take it at any opportunity, and even when no opportunity is present. The spiraling-down into the unconscious accompanying the lead-up to orgasm is a threshold of entry for a man into the mystery of life itself.

I recently blessed a relationship between a man and a woman who met in their retirement home at an advanced age. I have

---

44 Percy Bysshe Shelley, "Love's Philosophy," in Ernest Birnbaum, ed., *Anthology of Romanticism*, p. 873.

rarely seen two people so in love. I knew nothing of the particulars of their intimacy—it was none of my business—but I was
told that the man pursued the woman down the hall and that she
responded with pleasure, that he was psychologically potent regardless of his physical capacity. I could see that they gloried in
their intimacy.

What aspects of orgasm are specifically masculine? I know, of
course, that females also experience orgasm. But I am told that
it is not like male orgasm. For one thing, male orgasm is the goal
of every erection; it is the point of erection. That is less clear
about vaginal and clitoral excitement. Males are driven toward
orgasm to provide a release for millions of sperm pressing for
release, ejaculated in each climax. Their drive stamps masculinity with an unmistakable urgency. Female eggs do not press for a
goal. They wait for fecundation, a different kind of goal for the
egg. If fecundation does not happen, they drop away in men-
struation, having lost their chance. Male sperm do not so drop
away. They are reabsorbed into the tissues of the male, having
lost their chance to be sure, but also sure that the body's power
plant is churning up their successors.

For a male, orgasm begins early in puberty. Once a boy discovers it, he is no longer simply a boy however much he may
still be a boy. He has crossed a threshold. The threshold between
being a pubescent boy, with his early hint as to what is happening, the mystery of what is going on, and being male inevitably
involves heroic action—taking risks, searching for a knockout,
scheming and preparing for a winning streak, mastery, however
his phallic metaphor takes place. The core discovery is that his
penis is not just for peeing but also has a huge, intensive, self-
determining importance for him. He will not know just how huge
until he lives out a number of phallic episodes, when on some
occasion he gets the point. One such that I clearly remember was
a requirement in Boy Scout Troop 86 in St. Paul. In our primitive summer camp along the Sunrise River, some fifty miles
north of the city, each boy would walk up the hill toward the

local village cemetery, undress, with his clothes taken away, and stand naked there for some count. He would then find his way back to the campground in his altogether budding adolescence. Obviously the kid could not ask directions from a local farmhouse. I stood in that land of the dead for a time and at some point I decided that I'd had enough. I could not find my way back to camp. I don't recall how I managed—I suspect that I was eventually rescued by a counselor. What I have never forgotten is the initiatory heroic challenge and the humiliation—not to mention the cruelty of it.

The core physical element in classic phallic expression is friction, whether this be literal, which it is for the penis, or metaphorical, which it was for me in that cemetery. Each brings on and intensively anticipates orgasm. Physically, the rubbing of skin against skin brings the male into an intense expression of himself, anticipated by his innocent masturbation. Later, the purpose of friction dawns upon him and brings him into the *sine qua non* of masculine pleasure. Friction opens a male into a holding pattern for, and a wild anticipation of, a breathtaking ascension toward ecstasy. The farther he goes, the greater is his climb on the roller-coaster until he reaches an apex when there is no turning back.

No turning back

This "no turning back" element deserves comment. A crescendo of climax draws up from the bottom of a man's feet, ripples up his legs and explodes in his groin. It is, of course, possible to interfere with the process, to withdraw before ejaculation *(coitus interruptus)* or to move the extraordinary process into the psychic interior, as in Tantric exercises. But ordinarily, the excitement of impending orgasm has an authority unlike anything else the male body/psyche does. That in itself can give a man a strong clue about the importance of ecstasy.

Were the penetration resulting in fatherhood aimed at only the deposit of sperm, conception could be accomplished in an intentional and rational way, much as using a utensil in order to eat. The intense sensitivity of receptive flesh against erectile flesh invites wonderment, especially since the convulsive intensification of raging libido in intercourse sends a message to the body that is impossible to ignore: that to be a man is a wonderful thing.

What might be the point, the meaning, of not turning back . . the near undeniable subjective demand a man feels to go on to climax? My guess is that it is the beginning intimation, the inimitable precursor sign of ecstasy, the crossing of, yet again, a threshold, a barrier that stands between one's ego and the vast domain of the unconscious. Ecstasy is itself a mystery. It opens the door to a country that becomes ever more exquisitely available as the plot thickens. Ecstasy beckons from a far distance, promising and promising that which borders on eternal life—since one's progeny live on beyond one—colored by nuances of timelessness. It is as though a veil is drawn away—or as one analysand put it, "a valve opens," and the man, for the brief moment of his descent into the vortex, enters a hidden, always mysterious, reservoir of fulfillment. He sees, of course not with his eyes, but with a deeper vision, his eyes of faith, what Martin "saw" in his love affair with goat Sylvia, what Shelley "saw" in the mountains kissing high heaven, moonbeams kissing the sea.

The secret of life itself

It is no wonder that a man will not easily surrender contact with that reservoir of ecstatic union. Phallos is his key, unlocking his cask of treasure.

The only men—and perhaps women too, but that's another story—who will surrender the ecstasy that physical contact brings about are those who have found a similar explosion of intensity in a spiritual congress providing a similar plunge into what Jung called the *mysterium*. However, a problem with spiritually-dominated delight, reaching joyous inner dimensions, is that it can easily become ungrounded, separated from earthly reality, thereby diminishing a groundedness of the opposites in a union. Flesh is important to Christians due to the centrality of their belief in Christ's incarnation in the human Jesus. What a man's body and psyche aim to accomplish, subjectively, for him, under the aegis of ecstasy, is an approach, a pathway, to the exaltation of soul, the entrance to, an intimate closeness to, an initiation into what feels like the secret of life itself, even after hundreds of repetitions. The secret is not exposed in any concrete way; it is foretold, suggested, acted out even if in ignorance. I say again, a veil is lifted; an invitation to fulfillment is offered. Soul knows and soul follows a sense of the direction of body. A man moves, if but for an instant, into another—and another world. It drives a man out of his customary place, which is one aspect of its great promise.

That is every man's spiritual right and privilege and, were he to know it as such, his common experience with other men. It is presented to him within his natural phallic proclivity for entrance into a woman's body and in the spectacular fireworks, the paroxysm that takes place in him as he penetrates. Ecstasy is psychoid (about which more below). It is physical, of course, but it is, at the same time, of the psyche, invisible in the depths that it inculcates. It is tangibly intangible. A man moves into the precincts of the invisible world in his plunge into his lover's body. A male's proclivity for sex crosses the boundary between the opposites of spirit and matter. It is spiritual as much as it is physical.

Ego boundaries, difficult to establish and essential to hold to in adult consciousness, shimmer and become vague in the twilight zone of ecstatic orgasm. A man is driven out of his senses and into his lover. He is miles away from ecstasy if he thinks while having sex, which may be one of the factors in sexual abuse. A man might find no persuasive alternative to entering into his lover, which is why parents of teen-age girls are, with justification, so suspicious of their boyfriends. And especially young men, who can become mindless in their pubescence.

Consummation/sacrifice

The word used in referring to the coital establishment of marriage is that the marriage has been "consummated." That means that the man and woman have completed their union sexually, that they have joined together as a union of opposites, plighted their troth, moved out from singleness, taken psychological leave of their parents and ventured onto a new path together.

A woman's body is no longer only hers. A man's body—his phallic erection—is no longer only his. He vows to protect her as himself. She vows to protect him as herself. Such is the primary institution of the begetting of life in Western society. The two are joined together as if they were one. In point of symbolic truth, they *are* one; they are symbolically reconstituting their original human bisexuality in their union. The male projects his latent femininity upon the woman as she does her masculinity onto him. The hope of the community is that they will discover a depth in their love as they grow into their union, sharing both their disparate bodies and souls and their impending parenthood together. This is ambrosia: the most anyone might ask of another.

As they age together, leaving, for the most part, their youthful and surprising sexual exploits and parenthood in the past, something new can be born. Not so much children, but themselves as a unique entity. One can see the union of the sexes on the street, older people holding hands as they help one another cross, being kind to one another, worrying about each other, looking deeply within and without simultaneously. I sit on benches on Broadway in New York and other places where people walk and I observe this all the time. They could not know this as their fate at the point of their marriage. They can only know that they need or want a new life with each other. In age, they continue an erotic, even if no longer a genital, fascination for one another. They enter into a cosmic discovery which in age they give thanks for and celebrate as an accomplishment.

But passion, an ingredient of ecstasy, involves a man in suffering and in the sacrifice which passion suggests. For a male to stop going from female to female in the throes of phallic pleasure, always looking for new panoplies of ecstatic suggestion, new frictions, new substantiations of himself, to settle only on one female, is a masculine offering, a sacrifice. Women, I am sure, find it necessary to make a similar sacrifice. I am not one to say.

A man might perceive sex as an enemy of his phallic stature. He gives of himself but he is no longer himself, quite. Does he unconsciously resent his providing phallos to his lover? Does he unconsciously sense that he has lost his manhood in his penetration, that in entering virile and emerging spent, he is, as it were, castrated? Has he lost something important of himself? Is he, as the men said in my early days as a member of the Bemidji (MN) Lions' Club, "an exhausted rooster"? Phallos falls away; it plays itself out in manly work. It no longer rises to the occasion, lying there flaccid, a mere urination track, harmlessly wobbling back and forth with each step taken.

Sharon Olds, from whom I have gratefully borrowed much, leads me into still another consideration. For a man to share a woman's body in her adulthood, which, of course, he did as he was carried by his mother, is a recapitulation of a psychic ritual enclosed in physical form, touching hidden caverns of which he has no ego knowledge, returning, as it were, to his place of origin. A woman is starkly different from himself, a strange and often unsettling difference, which, if but for only a revelatory moment in his erotic history, can be his motivation for a lifetime of sensuous longing, always involving, in some way, the man's mother complex. Propelling his enterprise is the chthonic promise of bisexual and unitary wholeness, his need for repossession of a lost continent, his repair of ontological loneliness. All of this has huge mystic significance entailing a kind of surrender, including the loss of ego control in penetration, the loss of erection in age and after intercourse, without which the suffering of passion has but superficial meaning.

A man's loss of erection after intercourse suggests to him that he has disappeared. A woman physically loses nothing in intercourse, except her virginity in her first experience, however much she may lose emotionally. She does not become not a woman. A man loses his standard of maleness. He is no longer the heroic penetrator after orgasm. His standard, his hallmark, is gone. What he was in the strength of his beginning he has used. He is eaten alive by the female vagina at the moment of his greatest vulnerability. Might this be a psychological reason for why men have a fear of women and why necessary phallic aggression so often takes a hostile turn?

Once again, Sharon Olds, in her poem quoted above, points a direction with her use of the expression "consuming you." Consider the closeness of the word "consuming" to the Christian notion of the "consummation," the time of the end of all things in a fiery and final apocalyptic destruction when the Lord comes again. I do a double take.

Jung wrote of consummation only once that I know of, in a discussion of the Homilies attributed to the first-century St. Clement of Rome, namely:

> God unfolds himself in the world in the form of syzygies (paired opposites) such as heaven/earth, day/night, male/female, etc. . . At the end of this fragmentation process there follows the return to the beginning, the consummation of the universe through purification and annihilation.[45]

That means the end of ego and of consciousness. So it may be that what happens in sexual hunger and sacrifice is a reflection on the Biblical motif of consummation, as Olds suggests in looking at the animal world. Ecstasy, then, is the promise of, a taste of, the end of "fragmentation" in Jung's words, a portent of the end of gender separation, and at the same time the end of separated life as we know it. Seen in this light, for a man the

---

45 *Aion,* CW 9ii, par. 400.

"purification" of sexual union with a woman comes coupled with the "annihilation" of phallos as erect penetrator after ejaculation, ending in the loss of his power—limpness as opposed to potency, a sign of a new equality between the sexes.

Love between man and woman has the odor of sanctity hovering over it, overcoming barriers set between the two. The paradox is supreme: phallos, man's signature possession, his ownership of which is essential in the building of his inner grid,[46] is gone—if but suggestively—but enough gone to give him the shivers, to strike a note of danger. A man never knows that phallos's absence is temporary. After ejaculation, in a limp state, a man feels the pressure of Freud's *thanatos,* the death principle. Phallos annihilation connotes the sacrifice of ego intentionality in honor of soul (if it is genuine) in the offering of the man to the woman. Building manhood, critical as it is for a man, was never meant to be an end in itself in psyche. The end is the semblance of reunion, which comes when there are two developed opposites who offer their insularity, their self-sufficiency, to one another for their common good.

Secular/sacred

That which is secular is of the time, of history, of this world; in Jung's way, of the ego. It is perceived by two of Jung's four typological functions: thinking and sensation. That which is sacred is holy, of the other world, beyond time, more in tune with the other two functions: intuition and feeling. The sacred is beyond ego, which is why it is respected, whether in religion or in art. That, in Jung's terms, is the manifestation of the presence of the Self, regulating center of the psyche.

The sacred lies in the realm of mystery, of soul, of depth, of that which is held in the unconscious as, for example, in a sense of meaning. The problem in modern Western culture is that only thinking and sensation are considered to be valuable, signs of

---

46 See Monick, *Castration,* pp. 14f.

definition, signs of the dominance of patriarchy. Patriarchy is mistakenly perceived by men as the only way to masculine substance. But it leaves out the other two typological functions, feeling and, above all, intuition.

Ecstasy depends least of all on the thinking function, upon intuition most of all. When a man notices something of somatic erotic intuition arising within, entering his awareness, he knows that he must pay attention to its signaling, the flash of *gnosis* that surfaces. He enters a region of the holy, expressed, strangely to him, through his bodily, often-thought secular, faculties—his heart races, he trembles, his attention is distracted. His body cooperates with the unconscious. That moment of interior revelation, sending its signals to his body and to his chosen one, marks the prospective end of the sacred/secular dichotomy. The two are as one.

All sacred mystery finds its source within but becomes outwardly focused. A man becomes poised for action: phallos. He may hold back in the interest of strategy, in the interest of love, in respect, in fear, in obedience, in loyalty. All of these are ego decisions and often urgently important. But a certain die is cast however he decides. A man may become lost in the nectars of ambrosia, the secret of perfume, the dragnet of seduction, pulling him toward union. The signals of an opposite have been sent to his unconscious. All men are intrinsically religious, always on the edge of waiting for their soul to respond.

Ecstasy remains in a man's memory until the end, long after he is capable of enacting its rituals, just before he enters his final human pleroma. It is there for him even to this end, preparing him for what lies beyond. After puberty, a man comes to feel that he was made for this, the delights of penetration and its cosmic discovery; he finds that, in himself, he becomes a sacrament of body-soul, secular-sacred, ego-Self integration, what Edward F. Edinger called the ego-Self axis.[47] A man's erotic life is

---

47 See Edinger, *Ego and Archetype,* pp. 5ff.

his evidence of a soul, for his body responds to a soulful urgency.

The hidden background

Ecstasy reveals the hidden background of delight. It is hidden, I
suspect, due to the human need for discovery, which always,
even to the iron-clad rationalist, is a source of wonderment and
surprise. No man can know that he is a child of God, in the
strange language of the Church, without the discovery, within
himself, that he is capable of being surprised at the layers of
meaning that lie behind his everyday experience. Everyday can
be humdrum. With ecstasy as a given in every sexual encounter,
and thus as the backdrop of everyday, every day, every erection,
is revelation. Ecstasy means that the curtain can go up in a
man's theater. He may know the play in his head but he cannot
know how the director and actors will present it. Ecstasy is when
a new light goes on. It may show terror, it may show beauty, but
whether terror or beauty, or both, it is a delight to have the experience of knowing.

Ecstasy is the joy of knowing that another world stands behind the world of appearance, for men generally have limited
themselves only to this world. Finding oneself in that other
world, if only for the moment of ecstasy, can change a man's
life, as it obviously does. Phallos gives men that possibility.
Phallos does more. It suggests that we men move beyond appearance, beyond what we see in the bathroom mirror, to seek a
mental delight similar to what bodily delight suggests. Freud's
"pleasure" is too small a word for the encompassing enrichment
of ecstatic *gnosis.* Jung has no one word to describe the moment
of truth that comes with ecstasy. But we do not need Jung for
this. We can do it for ourselves. There is no substitute for that
moment of truth, when the scales fall from our eyes, the curtain
parts, and for a split second the secret of the universe is revealed. No wonder Teresa of Avila fainted.

Ecstasy sounds erudite. It is not. It is as common as male
sexuality, which we think of as suspicious. It is suspicious, of

course, since men are suspicious. But male sexuality is suggestive of human transcendence. The introduction happens when we see an interesting person, have designs, want a connection. We speak with our bodies and our bodies speak for our souls.

I write this with the hope that my brothers might find in themselves the brilliance of their sacramental nature and treasure it. A male is a holy being and he is so within a worldly guise, waiting to be revealed to himself and to a lover. Ecstasy is a way, a generic way, for a man to know his transcendence. It is a blessing. His debt is repaid in celebration and gratitude.

5

Spirit

Spirit as phallos; phallos as spirit

Jung assigned spirit to the realm of the masculine and the nature of *materia* as feminine. Given the importance of opposites in his thinking, he claimed that they have "always been [so] regarded."[48] Neither qualification can possibly be thoroughly true, however much cultural patriarchal propensities, Jung included, might claim otherwise. Jungian thinking speaks in useful yet problematic generalities, not in terms of specific people, who may vary from A to Z in their archetypal makeup. It speaks of typical patterns. It speaks of tendencies, not so much of absolutes. If one understands that, it is safe to continue. Patterns, especially important patterns, are necessary constructions in order that human beings might think, compare, construct.

Spirit, it seems to me, takes on its masculine flavor primarily in opposition to matter, as in spirit versus flesh. It is clearer today, more so perhaps than when Jung lived, that spirit and matter are no more ultimate, total opposites than are male and female, however much Jung depended upon gender as the quintessence of structural opposition. Masculine and feminine each contain elements of the other, as Jung well knew, in some males more of the feminine, in some males less, often due to conditioning in one's birth family. Jung used anima as a basic term denoting feminine aspects within the masculine psyche, as has been noted here earlier. An especially cogent notion of Jung's was his concept of the psychoid unconscious, which denotes a crossover transgressive quality in archetypal dimensions of the psyche where opposites, spirit and flesh, say, partake of qualities

---

48 *Mysterium Coniunctionis*, CW 14, par. 104.

of the other, as when the face of another person is seen to communicate a nonphysical message. Thus each trait has a way of also communicating its opposite. The point is that the division between spirit and flesh is not final. It is relative to what and when one "sees," what is seen, what is happening in the observer to condition the sight, and how the vision is interpreted.

As one delves more deeply into masculine psychology, one finds visible as well as invisible, rudimentary physical and psychic remnants of a primordially unified being, an urperson, as I have called it previously, as per Plato's original being. One can find expressions of such remnants in one's studies, in travels, in museum visits, and one can find them in oneself. For me, contact with *urperson* may be the reason I rise from my bed at 7 a.m. on Sunday and hie myself to the early Eucharist (it used to be to avoid the sermon, but unfortunately that can no longer be done) to connect with an approximation of original unity through ritual. Sacramental Christian worship, bread and wine/Body and Blood, God and human, the one opposite infused within the other, is the only widespread collective expression of transformation that exists in the West.

Spirit, co-existing and co-present with flesh beneath appearance, as in the psychoid unconscious, knowable only through the perception of mystery, is not worldly however strong its impact may be upon secular life, including a male's masculine apparatus. The reality beneath the accidents of the eucharistic ritual is invisible, lacking in all aspects of life that can be grasped only through the use of bodily sensation, as in *sub specie aeternitatis*. That does not make spirit less real than sensorily perceived data, although modern post-Enlightenment attitudes suggest the contrary. It takes subjective reflection, as spoken of here in the first chapter, quiet contemplation of pachysandra within, say, a deeper ritual context, exulting in child's play, searching into a partner's eyes, nudging the suspicion that they are his own eyes, sniffing out one's soul and one's partner's pubis, as a dog does, to get the drift. A man thereby crosses the threshold of becoming something of a new, or at least, a different, creature. Spirit is present.

So, in spite of their opposition, flesh, as in erection, is sponsored by and dependent upon spirit. In order to ponder the mystery of conjoining, it helps to name what is being conjoined, sometimes in as simplistic a way as if one were in a classroom taking novitiate notes. Typical masculine qualities, more strongly constellated in one man than in another, must be almost memorized through repetition in order for wisdom to gain a foothold.

Grasping the reality of mystery as it manifests itself in body goes against the grain of modern thinking. Recognizing mystery as one's own milieu demands a kind of conversion, a new way of seeing something that has been there all along—to understand deeply that body is psyche-like and spirit is body-like, as Marie-Louise von Franz once wrote. Making the body incorporeal and the spirit concrete expresses the paradox, opening the imagination to mystery. Body and spirit are not the same, clearly, yet each has a way of transmuting itself into the other, as phallos demonstrates in its transformation from urination tube to inseminator.

That, I think, is why pornography has always had power for men. Men can be mesmerized by it but it is actually the boy in the man, the boy in the tub, who is transfixed. Many men feel guilty about their interest in pornographic images or prose, but they need not. It is the natural consequence of their involvement in everything that pertains to phallos. The surge, the spasm of erotic energy that is stimulated in men by pornography, is a sign of the rapport between body and spirit, as the boy in the tub began to discover. A photograph, a film, approaches the soul as spirit, since there is psychic connection but no body connection, stimulating memory and desire, easily refracting into what Jung called a complex, pointing to a man's investment in body as instigator of soul.

I remember well that at the end of Barbara's and my "honeymoon" sojourn in Uganda, I crept into an urban park in Nairobi on our last day in East Africa, en route home, to take a photo of a woman chopping wood, which I had assiduously avoided doing until that last weak moment. Barbara stood on the road above. The woman saw me at the last minute and turned on me with her machete. I ran for my life with Barbara convulsed in laughter. Innocent me. Innocent Barbara. I remember as well the scene in the film *Apocalypse Now* as the soldiers in a helicopter receiving fire removed their helmets and placed them over their groins. And, yet again, in Stephen Ambrose's *D-Day,*

> "Where are the damn mine fields?" the [American] officer shouted [at the German prisoners]. With an arrogant look on his face, the prisoner gave his name, rank and serial number. The American fired his carbine between the German's knees. With a smirk on his face, the German pointed to his crotch and said, "*Nicht hier.*" Then he pointed to his head and said, "*Hier!*"
>
> The American interrogator gave up and waved the prisoner away. Slaughter [the American observer, interestingly named] commented, "This convinced me that we were fighting first-rate soldiers."[49]

However it is that spirit is present in all persons, as is body, spirit's affinity to the masculine is, as written, as serious a component of gender separation as phallos and vagina. To repeat, all physical life, all birth, all crops from the earth, all fish from the sea, originate in the Mother. There is no other source of origin aside from male cooperation. Males are an essential element in bringing forth new life but males are far from the basic element. They are far more than an accessory, an adjunct, an auxiliary, but still they are secondary. It may be that in the future conception will take place commonly, even as it is today exceptionally, without the benefit of penetrating phallos. But for millennia, no other way was possible and it is from that kind of universal human experience that archetypes have been born and are alive today in the psyche.

---

49 *D-Day,* p. 460.

Yet auxiliary status for men is as insufficient and dangerous in life as it is for women under patriarchy. Such secondary placement of the masculine invites the kind of compensation evident in patriarchy. There is hardly a way to avoid such a danger save in a new way of understanding masculinity. Spirit asserts masculinity in manifold symbolic and metaphorical ways and does so without demeaning the feminine. While there is a certain logic in one's thinking of spirit as "belonging" to the masculine side of the gender divide, a careless or doctrinaire assignment of spirit to masculinity is not only untrue but brings no psychic equilibrium to the war of the sexes. So doing creates the possibility of continuing patriarchal domination.

"You can't have phallos without spirit"

Here I need to retell a story I first told in *Phallos: Sacred Image of the Masculine*.[50] When I was a relatively fresh analyst in New York, just before *Phallos* was published, the Analytical Psychology Club of New York invited me to speak on the subject. The Club's public lectures have always been a way for analysts to try out their new works and are an important contribution to the development of Jungian thought. I imagine many analysts came to my lecture because I was speaking on a topic Jungians usually shy away from, preferring to leave sex to Freud, as it were, and because I was new in New York and had trained in Zürich and they wanted to see what they had.

I was nervous and stayed close to my script. One of those present was Erlo Van Waveren, an older therapist who had himself studied for years in Zürich. At the midpoint break, he rose up with some vehemence and called out: "Mr. Monick, where is the spirit? You can't have phallos without spirit!" I was dumbfounded, of course, but then I was struck with a stroke of genius (spirit?), largely due to my ten years as vicar of St. Clement's, an experimental theater-political congregation off Times Square,

---

50 *Phallos*, p. 82.

where I was required to improvise at a moment's notice. I laughed at his catching me in my speaking of phallos in a phallic-less stance and then, putting the manuscript aside, told Van Waveren that he was right. I spoke enthusiastically and extemporaneously, which I could have done at the beginning, as he suspected, had I the confidence. Van Waveren had made his point, I had accepted it and from that moment he calmed down and the presentation went smashingly.

It occurs to me now and for the first time that Van Waveren's explosion bears a resemblance to a girl's father walking into the house just as a young man might be getting into serious business with the daughter. The young man may crumble when he is discovered, but he would never have gotten to the point of crumbling had he no beginning soulful confidence in himself.

Here we see a conflict between nature and culture. Confidence-building is crucial to a man's use of his phallic nature and comes into being inspired by a male's own inner masculine grid, grid being my word for the interior, archetypal testosterone-based structure of masculine identity.[51] Without phallos operating from within his grid, a man can be at a loss as what to do in his girlfriend's living room before her father walks in. The father knows his own grid and projects this, accurately, onto the boy's intention. The *gnosis* both of them have, the medium for the projection, is spirit. The boy's connection to spirit begins in his oedipal realization that he is a breed apart from his mother, that he has a fate separate from hers and that his personal discovery of that fate gives him strength, importance, invigoration, which is to say, potency. He can find that fate only through his own experience of loyalty to his maleness.

I have come to understand that the connection between phallos and spirit becomes apparent when a man allows phallos to be his metaphoric and spiritual guide. Not physical erection exactly, although erection is an essential signifier of spirit's

---

51 See Monick, *Castration,* pp. 20f.

presence, but physical erection also as understood to be translated into symbolic phallos—strong, aimed at its target, intense, firm, intrusive, self-confident, lacking self-doubt, unable not-to-risk, wanting to lead—as in the sculpture pictured on the cover of this book. The intensity of spirit in males is an extension of the intensity of erection. That was Van Waveren's point. He was saying, "Don't hide behind your notes, Monick. Let us see what you have."

It goes without saying that phallos, actually or symbolically, cannot be waved about indiscriminately. That is the patriarchal way, which is doomed as more men become conscious, and because women will not take it anymore.

The sacredness of spirit

As I was writing this chapter, I overheard my wife say, in a telephone conversation with our London daughter, " . . . you are such a good Mom." I thought to myself, not for the first time, that, whether affirmative or not, parenting never ends. It is built into the continuing pattern of human life. No one makes up the pattern; it comes with the human condition. This kind of moment illustrates Jung's concept of a religious man, one who lives "the life of the careful observer" (op.cit. p.72), quite aside from what others may think of the value of what he observes. It might be said that my making that connection is an example of careful observation. For me, its spiritual importance stems from Jung's comment on one trait of a religious man, that one cannot be a religious man without spirit. Hence noticing is a spiritual activity.

Why is that? Spirit is of the ephemeral, the non-rational, of feeling, of intuition. Spirit becomes apparent through sensibility, as when it becomes part of one's awareness from out of the blue. That last phrase is a common way of referring to intuition, suggesting that whatever one is referring to comes from outside of ego consciousness. It is difficult to prove the existence of spirit. It is no wonder that early humans did not connect the phallic spurt in intercourse to the wonder of conception. It comes in a flash and in sexual congress—no one sees it. In an instant, it disappears into the woman. In time, her pregnancy becomes visible. He just gets up and goes to the hunting grounds. Masculine invisibility, in that sense, is built into the game. To stretch a point, there is a correspondence between maleness and spirit, maleness and invisibility, which is probably implicit in my cocking an ear to my wife's telephone conversation with my daughter. It may not be stretching the matter too far to wonder about the correspondence between the invisibility of spirit and the invisibility of the male's effectual contribution to on-going human life. Perhaps that is one reason men put such a premium on visible potency.

All of the above circumambulates the question of spirit, sacredness and potency. What I have attempted to do is to encourage respect for masculinity on the basis of four aspects of phallic importance as opposed to patriarchal dominance, the most common measure of self-worth men have. Spirit, since it is invisible, is more difficult to correlate with phallos than the first three (fatherhood, union, ecstasy), all of which have participation in the body. Yet the cause is not lost. Women desire and need the male body, but often they fall in love with a man toward whom they do not have an erotic response, finding only later that their admiration extends to his member. Even when it doesn't, she may continue to embrace him. A man who depends only upon physical phallos can be a man who loses the attraction he has, since the spirit of manliness, as in protection, will not be communicated through his personality. Manliness must have the dimension of spirit, as in husbandry, provision, care, which is never communicated by means of domination or demand. Aggression is not missing, for aggression in the cause of defending family, love, responsibility and civility is an implication and metaphor of phallos. Aggression as an assertive, bold and enterprising note, can be not only a manifestation of phallos, but also a major evocation of spirit, joining the man and his lover in an enduring collusion.

One who loves a man of spirit senses his sacred quality. He evokes wonder. He has moved somewhere beyond self-interest, at least in a significant part of himself. Essentially, he can be trusted.

D-Day 2004

Barbara's and my three-month stint in London in 2004 coincided with the sixtieth anniversary of the Allied D-Day invasion of France. That timing dominated our stay, next to our daughter's family and the writing of this book. Our friend Paulette Goldstein of Paris and New York, with the help and enthusiasm of her French friends Jeanine and Claude Audinnot, organized a visit to Normandy for the observances. Barbara and I went to the superb London Imperial War Museum twice, I read Stephen Ambrose's *D-Day,* a huge, masterful volume of day-to-day, beach-to-beach, unit-to-unit history and evaluation. I read, as well, extensive coverage of the historic landings and anniversary events in the newspapers, which I was excited by and devoured. I was in search of spirit in the men who fought and died there, sick from the sea, scared out of their wits, open to fire from the cliffs. I found it.

Here are some passages from Ambrose's book:

Tired as he must have been, Ramsey [the British Naval Commander-in-Chief of the landings] caught *the spirit and soul* of the great undertaking perfectly. (p. 195, italics added)

Sgt. Elmo Jones of the 505th PIR [parachute regiment] jumped at 300 feet or so. Just before exiting the C-47 he said a brief prayer: "Lord, Thy will be done. But if I'm to die, please let me die like a man." (p. 196)

Not many of them [American troops] were there by choice. Only a few of them had a patriotic passion they would speak about. But nearly all of them would rather have died than let down their buddies or look the coward in front of their bunkmates. (p. 167)

> The exemplary manner in which they seized their opportunity, their dash, boldness, initiative, teamwork and tactical skills were outstanding beyond praise. (p. 352)

> Pvt. Robert Zafft, a twenty-year-old infantryman . . . put his feelings and experience this way: "I made it up the hill, I made it all the way to where the Germans had stopped us for the night, and I guess I made it up the hill of manhood." (p. 581)

Spirit among the fighting men of D-Day was a crucial element in the Allied success. Many of the Nazi soldiers were exhausted, especially if they had come from the Eastern front, as many had. Many were older men and very young schoolboys, since the Soviet front had consumed millions of Germany's disciplined military. Many were enforced conscriptees from overrun Eastern European nations with no interest in fighting Americans. Many were bored and lethargic occupiers of France, where nothing of consequence had happened for years. They were, however, dug-in and heavily entrenched defenders of coastal France where, in many ways, the Nazi armies had strategic advantage.

The German forces did not have psychological advantage. The Americans at Omaha and Utah beaches and the British and Canadians somewhat farther north along the same coast had the leverage of a cause they believed in and which most of the world ardently believed in too. Green as many of them were, after long waits on sea from North America, and in England, they were restless to move, in spite of almost universal seasickness crossing a rough Channel. They were well trained and prepared—although nothing can adequately prepare one for a fortified beach invasion. And they had waited a long time. Spirit hung in their midst. It came out of them and it descended upon them.

The Allied spiritual advantage was their need to topple Hitler and their belief in the moral necessity of their victory. The Allied forces were young and battle-fresh in spite of the sea. They believed even when they did not believe: their lives and their pride as representatives of civilization were at stake. They embarked on the shores of Normandy as a first assault and they were determined not to let their cohorts down. That is spirit as found in men. Men support men; they need brotherhood, they need collaboration. The greatest sea invasion in history could not have happened without serious cooperation among the multitudes and layers of men who jumped out of their landing crafts into the face of gunfire, who jumped from planes, who survived the glider landings, who did not know where they were in a foreign land. They held on in spite of confusion, fog, smoke and the horrendous noise of bombs and naval shelling, the dead bodies and grisly slaughter of those about them.

"The cruelty, wastefulness and stupidity of war"

Thank God for the *International Herald Tribune* and for the fact that Barbara reads it even more carefully than I do. The day after the sixtieth anniversary of the Normandy landings she found John S. D. Einsenhower's article, "War turned invasion's overall commander into a pacifist."[52] I was deeply moved by that, our second visit to the beaches and the cemeteries, the old soldiers, sailors and paratroopers we met at Pointe-du-Hoc and Ste.-Mère-Église. People who did not fight talked a lot. The veterans were more quiet. I myself was reduced to an almost reverential silence and an enormous desire to contemplate and meditate and to be alone, especially on the sands at the new Omaha Beach memorial sculpture.

I had been a beginning high school student in St. Paul in 1944 (the same age as many of the German military assigned to Normandy, as it turned out), greatly fascinated by the war but far from any actual involvement, aside from an uncle by marriage who was killed in the invasion of Italy. I think, now, that my adolescent fascination had not only to do with phallic bombing, bombardment and our side's winning, but with the bravado demonstrated by the men who were there. Many American soldiers

---

52 June 7, 2004, p. 10.

in the war were only slightly older than I, more ready than I for a challenge of that sort. Many, I am sure, were short of a first seriously erotic kiss, just as I was. Danger lurks in an erotic kiss, especially an early one. One can lose one's ego stability to the pressures coming from a suddenly liberated unconscious. War is dangerous. One can lose one's life before one even knows what is happening. Spirit, eros and death intersect.

As a student born into a Midwestern [Teddy Roosevelt] Republican family, I was an enthusiastic supporter of President Eisenhower, both in college and seminary, aided and abetted by having lived under Democratic presidents almost since I was born. (Today I cannot imagine my not voting for Adlai Stevenson). As I remember Ike, the most radical thing that came from him was his general warning about the dangers to America from the military-industrial complex, which would press for war preparation as a means of attaining profit. That should have given me a clue had my growing liberal mind been a bit more liberal. He was, to my conventional mind, a genuine American hero.

But Ike a pacifist? I would like to know what happened to John Eisenhower, his son, himself a West Point graduate, to characterize his father, arguably America's greatest general and twice its Republican president, as a pacifist:

> The most fundamental conviction that the period of Ike's command in Europe and the Mediterranean imprinted on his mind was the *cruelty, wastefulness, and stupidity of war*.[53]

That suggests to me that patriarchy has been dealt a blow. That is enough, in itself, to establish one man's connection to spirit, at least as spirit manifests in a humane direction. Spirit moves one sideways from what one is trained to do, what one is expected to do, even what one expects himself to be and do and into a place that is personally and, I would say, mystically, one's

---

53 Ibid.(italics added).

own. Do I claim here that Ike was a mystic? In a conventional sense, no. In the sense that I have proposed in this book, and if his son John is correct, it is likely that Ike moved in a mystical direction, that he listened to an interior spirit and became obedient to it, leaving behind the soldier he was trained to be. How else could he move in a direction so opposed to his history and accomplishments? Something serious had to have happened to him, something at the core of his being.

I wonder if Ike was a man who looked into himself and found a subjective conflict between his soul and that which made him the most celebrated general of World War Two. John Eisenhower was himself a man who graduated from West Point like his father, trained there for the military life. He grew up with a father who inculcated a respect for tradition, authority and strategy. That Ike might allow a radical change in his mind and sensibility about the efficacy of war, bespeaking generosity, compassion and independence, I call the presence of spirit in him. The possibility that a man, and especially one not known for high intellect or sacred interests, can move toward a humanitarian attitude, evinces the presence of a transcendent provenance which the Church has called grace. Men often stop their growth at a point called "conditioning." Extraordinary men find within themselves the capacity to be inspired.

A man's calling everything he has learned about military proficiency, culminating in war, "stupidity" is, from my position as a Christian, an act of grace. From my Jungian standpoint, John Eisenhower's evaluation of his father is an example of individuation, "a person's becoming himself, whole, indivisible and distinct from other people or collective psychology."[54] Ike is commonly considered to be a sort of regular guy, no great shakes as a president, much like the rest of us except for an extraordinary ability as a military leader. His pacifist sympathies after the war came as an enormous surprise to me. That element of sur-

---

54 Samuels et al, eds., *A Critical Dictionary*, p. 76.

prise is in keeping with both masculine identity and spirit. One's individuation is a private matter, particularly when one is an introvert, as I suspect Ike was. It has to do with the impact of the world first upon a man's soul and then, consequently, upon his mind. One cannot easily discuss the condition of one's soul. That does not mean that nothing is happening. It may be that the general public will know of a famous man's inner transitions only after some sixty years, if ever, and even then not as he told it. Spirit is an aspect of a man's life about which even he may be mute, but my God, the transition from being a warrior to being a pacifist—it is strangely similar to Ignatius of Loyola, who himself had been a military man. I can imagine Ike saying, "It's just common sense, knowing war as I do."

Vigor

In contrast to the receptive and nurturing qualities of the feminine, masculinity suggests another kind of energy— robustness, strength, forcefulness, vitality, toughness—all primary characteristics of potency. Spirit is, as Van Waveren insisted, inherently implicated in the notion and symbol of phallos. Impotence, basically the inability to have or maintain an erection, or loss of phallos, is from Latin *impotens* meaning "loss of power" (see next chapter). I have thought, in stronger moments, that erection is, for men, "the voice of God in one's loins." If that is anything more than pseudo-poetic romanticism, phallos as masculine trait is sacred and its vigor—for there is no phallos without vigor, a sign of spirit—is a sign of the presence of the divine in man.

Vigor and spirit are inseparable. A man's vigor can survive him only if he gives evidence of its presence before his death. The hero comes to mind. A hero stands against odds where a weaker man might fold; a hero is victorious; a hero, expressing phallos, is a demigod, since he overcomes impediments with his more-than-ordinary bravery and courage and his "magic instrument." Phallos morphs into a man's personality characteristics, making him vigorous. Spirit spurts from vigor. Ejaculation is a sacrament of vigor. Hundreds of thousands of spermatozoa die en route to the ovaries. One succeeds. If ever there were a hero, that guy is it.

As I write this I read in the *New York Times* an article titled "The Renewal of Life on the Edge of Death." It is the story of Tom Andrews and Marisol Velasco—she is a woman but what an animus she has!—climbing El Capitan in Yosemite National Park in California. A ferocious storm assaults them as they are camped for the night on a rock ledge four feet by three feet [for two people!] two hundred feet below the summit on that formidable rock. She writes in her journal:

> The danger is not imagined. At any moment, a giant chunk of rock or ice could be washed off the top and cleave us from the wall. Our fear of death is not what's getting to us now; it is the duration of that fear that is eating away at our morale . . . we are exhausted, wet and shivering. In about an hour it will be nightfall, the temperature will drop and we will die.[55]

They are rescued. Tom Andrews says, "I have been asked if this ordeal has soured my desire to climb. I have to say no. This sport has presented me with so many gifts: a sense of self, community and friendships to last a lifetime," not the least of whom is Marisol, "my partner, my hero, my friend."

Spirit. Andrews projects onto his companion his own inner qualities, doubtless with an enormous hook on which to hang the projection, as no doubt she also did with him. Their extremely dangerous situation, their awareness of the perilous closeness of death, their tenacious intention to hold on to their miniscule perch, is testimony (and the word testimony has its root in Latin *testes*) to the presence of spirit. They came close to defeat but not because of loss of vigor. They were never impotent.

Vigor spurts from spirit.

---

55 April 24, 2005, section 8, p. 11.

A letter from a reader

The end of this book has nearly come. What have I left out that should be in this small but decade-long effort? I once again take out my file on "spirit" and thumb through its many notes, clippings, dreams and quotations. I find a stashed-away, valued letter from a reader of my two earlier books, Andrew Olivo of Oregon. This is what I was looking for without knowing it. He wrote:

> I have always, since a very young age, been aware of the spirituality inherent in having an erection. It is a feeling of potency, a feeling of having the awesome ability to create life, a feeling of being completely alive—perhaps the closest a man can come to what a woman feels in being pregnant or giving birth. Odd, then, that it is such a degraded and maligned experience in our culture. . . . Do you think that perhaps it could be seen by some men as "feminine" to think of erection as spiritual?

I think that men generally distrust the inside, the soul, as being antagonistically feminine, especially men who have not had a clear outcome of their oedipal struggle. Their mother and the archetypal Mother are still, psychologically, at large within them, the enemy, expecting, even demanding, an obedience to herself and not to the deep roots of her son's masculinity. Perhaps this is another reason why spirit is seen by Jungians as masculine. How does a man resist the seduction of the deep sleep of release in death on, say, El Capitan except by a refusal to give in . . . to hold out on the ledge against the odds. What gives him the impulse to do this? Is it a recrudescence of the anti-oedipal energy of his childhood? That he does so with a woman is quite amazing. Yet every potent man follows that path.

So, that's it for now—my fantasy of fatherhood, the union of opposites, ecstasy and spirit, as seen from within a man's psychological, subjective, mystical/erotic reality, comes to an end. Ah, but this is only a beginning.

La Grande Boucle (The Big Loop),
honoring the Tour de France.
(Sculpture by Bernard Métais, near Pau, France.)

6

A Note on Impotence

An antithesis of potency is, of course, impotence—a man's inability to attain an erection or maintain one for sexual excitement and intercourse. Impotence comes upon a man primarily from two sources: physical impediments, including age and illness, and psychological interference with a natural process. It always manifests itself as a shadow, or negative (from the ego's standpoint) aspect of masculine life. Since this work does not dwell on the negative, I can give here only a short piece of imagination to impotence, just to even the score in a work that celebrates penetration.

My mind races to James Hillman, to my mind the apogee of Jungian analysts who find a certain strain of truth in paradoxical equivalences, taking Jung's respect for neurosis and the negativity of a good God into the depths of the unconscious. As I write this, I am reading his latest—and, he says, his last—book, *A Terrible Love of War*. I hate war, though I have never been in one, maybe like men hate impotence (I have been in that, and have not loved it, but maybe that helps me understand Hillman.) But Hillman finds himself, not loving war, but understanding how men can love war and finding in himself a certain respect for it. "War begs for meaning,: he writes, "and amazingly also gives meaning."[56]

So what meaning might be found in impotence? I can think of three points to make.

1) No matter how my muscles might stand out and how much I might like to ogle women, I am an aging man headed to the end of life as I know it. Impotence tells me that. The stand-up quality of phallos belongs to youth, the time of life where one has

---

56 *A Terrible Love of War*, p. 10.

the energy to raise children and for me that is gone. I take pills each day for my diabetes. Diabetes produces vascular problems and vascular problems bring on impotence.

Impotence leads me into that kind of reflection. It invites and broadens my mystical awareness. But it does not diminish my memory. I have not forgotten what makes me a man. In fact, its absence helps me to value what I have had and still, in a puny way, have,

2) My difficulty in having strong erections helps me to pay a somewhat different kind of attention to women, including my wife. They—and she—attract me in new ways. Being with them takes on a newish resonance. I don't like to travel any more but sometimes I travel nonetheless because Barbara does. We have fun and we like discovering new things together, like we used to in sex. Sex is the foundation of our enjoyment of each other even as phallos and vagina become life-metaphors. We do this in our reading and our film watching and we get more out of what we watch together—we even hate the same movies, something we never paid any attention to. I am beginning to think that our book discussions, sparked by the *New York Review of Books*—her mainstay, my discovery—are a kind of elder-intimacy. I understand Barbara's love of family better than ever. She better understands my political urgency, particularly my concern over the composition of the U.S. Supreme Court. She may even forgive my election intrusion that time in the hospital.

3) My deprivation—when it is there—nudges my awareness of the importance of what is gone and what will be further gone when Barbara is gone and/or I am gone. And what is still here. It encourages my treasuring of memory and my intensity of conviction. For a male, erection and life are concomitant, whether remembered or presently experienced. That, however, does not mean that absence is total absence. Here is where Hillman helps. I suspect that inside Hillman is the suspicion that the loss of life in war (for me, read erection) is the beginning of a new life. Surely that has been true for him as a philosophical writer.

Gratitudes

In no order of preference, or any other order, except for the first three, and aside from many teachers and analysands, toward whom I feel great respect and gratitude, I wish to thank

Barbara Monick
Stephen Monick
Katherine Monick Hogarth
Marc Lippman
Christopher Reynolds
Alice Petersen
Nancy Qualls-Corbett
John Desteian
G. Marcel Martin
Diana Grace-Jones
Jean Green
Judith Gleason
Janet Dallett
Melissa Werner
Paul Stein
William Davis
Paulette Goldstein
Michael Steffen
Louise Mullen
Douglas Price
Andrew Olivo
Paul Coviello
John McDonnell
George Schemel, SJ
John Willen
Laurence Beasley

Bibliography

Ambrose, Stephen. *D-Day*. New York: Touchstone, 1994.

Ankori, Micha. "A Mytho-Psychological Study of the Biblical Legacy." In *Journal of Jungian Theory and Practice*. New York: C.G. Jung Institute of New York, vol. 7, no. 1 (2005).

Bataille, Georges. *Eroticism*. San Francisco: City Lights Books, 1986.

Birnbaum, Ernest. *Anthology of Romanticism*. New York: The Ronald Press Company, 1948.

Bly, Robert; Hillman, James; Meade, Michael; eds. *The Rag and Bone Shop of the Heart*. New York: HarperCollins, 1992.

Book of Common Prayer. The Church of England. Cambridge, UK: Cambridge University Press: n.d.

Calasso, Robert. *The Marriage of Cadmus and Harmony*. New York: Alfred A. Knopf, 1993.

Campbell, Joseph. *The Hero With a Thousand Faces*. Cleveland: Meridian/World Publishing, 1967.

Chia, Mantsk. *Taoist Secrets of Love—Cultivating Male Sexual Energy*. New York: Aurora Press, 1984.

Colman, Arthur and Colman, Libby. *The Father*. Wilmette, IL: Chiron, 1988.

Conroy, Frank. *Dogs Bark, But the Caravan Rolls on: Observations Then and Now*. New York: Houghton Mifflin, 2002.

Corneau, Guy. *Absent Fathers, Lost Sons*. Boston: Shambhala, 1991.

Crenshaw, Theresa. *The Alchemy of Love and Lust*. New York: G. P. Putnam's Sons, 1996.

Countryman, L. William. *Dirt, Greed, and Sex: Sexual Ethics in the New Testament and Their Implications for Today*. Philadelphia: Fortress Press, 1988.

Daniélou, Alain. *The Phallus*. Rochester, VT: Inner Traditions, 1995.

De Castillejo, Irene Claremont. *Knowing Woman*. New York: G. P. Putnam's Sons, 1973.

Dworkin, Andrea. *Intercourse.* New York: The Free Press, 1987.

Edinger, Edward F. *The Aion Lectures: Exploring the Self in Jung's* Aion. Toronto: Inner City Books, 1996.

_____. *Ego and Archetype.* New York: G. P. Putnam's Sons, 1972.

_____. *The Mysterium Lectures: A Journey through Jung's* Mysterium Coniunctionis. Toronto: Inner City Books, 1995.

Elie, Paul. *The Life You Save May Be Your Own.* New York: Farrar, Straus amd Giroux, 2003.

_____. *The History of Sexuality,* vol. I. New York: Vintage Books, 1980.

Friedman, David M, *A Mind of Its Own.* New York: The Free Press, 2001.

Gleason, Judith. *Sentinels of the Earth,* video. New York: Women Make Movies, 2001.

Griffiths, Bede, OSB. *A Human Search*, video. Sydney, Australia: More than Illusion Films, 1993.

Harding, M. Esther. *The I and the Not-I: A Study in the Development of Consciousness* (Bollingen Series LXXIX). Princeton: Princeton University Press, 1973.

Harris, Robert. *Pompeii.* London: Hutchinson, 2003.

Hillman, James. *A Terrible Love of War.* New York: Penguin Books, 2004.

Hillman, James, and Livernois, Jay. *Archetypal Sex.* Woodstock, CT: Spring, 1995.

Hollis, James. *Under Saturn's Shadow.* Toronto: Inner City Books, 1994.

John of the Cross. *The Dark Night of the Soul.* New York: Riverhead Books (Penguin Putnam), 2003.

Kerényi, Carl. *Dionysos.* Princeton, NJ: Princeton University Press, 1976.

Jaffé, Aniela. *Was C.G. Jung A Mystic?* Einsiedeln, Switzerland: Daimon Verlag, 1989.

Jones, Steve. *Y:The Descent of Men.* New York: Houghton Mifflin, 2003.

Jung, C.G. *The Collected Works* (Bollingen Series XX). 20 vols. Trans.

R.F.C. Hull. Ed. H. Read, M. Fordham, G. Adler, Wm. McGuire. Princeton: Princeton University Press, 1953-1979.

_____. *Memories, Dreams, Reflections.* Ed. Aniela Jaffé, trans. Richard and Clara Winston. New York: Pantheon Books, 1963.

Keuls, Eva. *The Reign of the Phallus.* New York: Harper and Row, 1985.

Lacan, Jacques. *Feminine Sexuality.* New York: W. W. Noton, 1982.

McGill, Michael. *Male Intimacy. New York:* Harper and Row, 1985.

McGuire, William, and Hull, R.F.C., eds. *C.G. Jung Speaking: Interviews and Encounters* (Bollingen Series XCVII). Princeton: Princeton University Press, 1977.

Miller, Geoffrey. *The Mating Mind.* London: William Heinemann, 2000.

Moore, Thomas. *Care of the Soul.* New York: Harper Perennial, 1994.

Moore, Thomas. *The Soul of Sex.* New York: HarperCollins, 1998.

Monick, Eugene. *Castration and Male Rage.* Toronto: Inner City Books, 1991.

_____. *Evil, Sexuality and Disease in Grünewald's Body of Christ.* Dallas, TX: Spring Publications, 1993.

_____. *Phallos: Sacred Image of the Masculine.* Toronto: Inner City Books, 1987.

Néret, Gilles. *Erotica Universalis.* Cologne: Benedikt Taschen, 1994.

Olds, Sharon. "Greed and Aggression." In Bly, Robert; Hillman, James; Meade, Michael; eds. *The Rag and Bone Shop of the Heart.* New York: HarperCollins, 1992.

Otto, Rudolf. *The Idea of the Holy.* Oxford: The Oxford University Press, 1958.

Polanyi, Michael. *Personal Knowledge.* Chicago: University of Chicago Press, 1958.

Priapea: Poems for a Phallic God. Trans. W. H. Parker. London: Croom Helm, 1988.

Ryce-Menuhin, Joel. *Naked and Erect.* Wilmette, IL: Chiron, 1996.

Rumi, *The Essential Rumi.* Trans. Coleman Barks. New York: HarperSanFrancisco, 2004.

Samuels, Andrew, Shorter, Bani, Plaut, Fred. *A Critical Dictionary of Jungian Analysis.* London: Routledge & Kegan Paul, 1986.

Samuels, Andrew, ed. *The Father.* New York: New York University Press, 1986.

Shelley, Percy Bysshe. "Love's Philosophy." In *Anthology of Romanticism.* Ed. Ernest Birnbaum. New York: The Ronald Press Company, 1948.

Stevens, Anthony. A*rchetype Revisited: An Updated Natural History of the Self.* Toronto: Inner City Books, 2003..

Swofford, Anthony. *Jarhead.* New York: Scribner, 2003.

Tatham, Peter. *The Making of Maleness.* London: Karnac Books, 1992.

Telechea , José Idígoras. *Ignatius of Loyola: The Pilgrim Saint.* Trans. Cornelius Buckley. Chicago: Loyola University Press, 1994.

Te Paske, Bradley A. *Rape and Ritual: A Psychological Study.* Toronto: Inner City Books, 1982.

Touching the Void (film). Independent Film Channel, UK, 2004.

Underhill, Evelyn. *Essentials of Mysticism.* London: J.M. Dent and Sons, 1920.

_____. *Light of Christ.* London: Longmans, Green & Co., 1944.

_____. *Mysticism.* London: Methuen, 1911.

von Franz, Marie-Louise. *Alchemy.* Toronto: Inner City Books, 1980.

Vogt, Gregory Max. *Return to Father.* Dallas, TX: Spring Publications, 1991.

Wright, Robert. *The Moral Animal: The New Science of Evolutionary Psychology.* London: Abacus, 1996.

Wylie, James. *The Phallic Quest.* Toronto: Inner City Books, 1989.

Index

Page numbers in *italics* refer to illustrations

153

intuition, 8
Iraq, 18

Jung, C.G./Jungian(s), 9-14, 29, 32-36, 56,
    61, 67, 70-71, 75, 83, 86-87, 95, 97,
    101, 110, 113, 127, 129, 141, 144
    Aion, 124
    "Answer to Job," 17
    four functions, 125
    Mysterium Coniunctionis, 109, 114
    on neurosis, 62, 73
    on religion, 74
    "The Symbolic Life," 72-74

Kabbalah, 15
knowledge, absolute, 95-97
Kotschnig, Elined, 31

letter, 144
liberal, 25
logos, 16, 36
loneliness, 73, 75, 123
looking vs. seeing, 53

male(s)/maleness, 7, 34, 36, 45, 48, 55-56,
    58, 62, 107. *See also* masculine/
    masculinity; phallos
manliness, *see* male(s)/maleness;
    masculine/masculinity; phallos
marking(s), 68
marriage, 19, 41-43, 92, 99, 105, 121
masculine/masculinity, 7, 9, 15, 23, 26, 31-
    32, 34, 37, 41, 45, 48-50, 60, 64-66,
    71, 84, 86, 108, 110, 112-113, 118,
    123, 129-130, 132-134, 136, 142,
    144, 146. *See also* male(s)/maleness;
    phallos
    four ways into, 32, 36-43,136
masturbation, 27, 51, 64, 108, 119
matter, 32-33, 60, 121, 129
meaning, 27, 127
meditation garden, 77
Métais, Bernard: *La Grande Boucle,* 45-
    46, *145*

metapsychology, 35-36, 50, 54, 60
Mexico, 68-69
Michelangelo, 9
mindfulness, 92
Monick, Barbara, 41-43, 79-80, 91
moon, 53-55
mother/mothering, 32-33, 37, 47-48, 87,
    89, 97-99, 101, 123, 132, 134, 144
mountain climbing, 143-144
mysterium tremendum, 72-76
mystery, 8, 13, 23, 25-26, 28, 34, 42, 44,
    51, 53-54, 59, 62, 72, 76, 86, 98, 120,
    125-126, 130
mystic/mystical/mysticism, 14-15, 22, 24,
    26, 45, 50, 54, 62-63, 65, 71-72, 109,
    140-141

natural/nature, 23, 47, 57-59, 62-63, 97,
    113
neurosis, 62, 73
new life, 9
no turning back, 119-120
numen/numinosum, 14, 59-61, 63

obligations of fatherhood, 84. *See also*
    responsibilities of fatherhood
Olds, Sharon, 123
    "Greed and Aggression," 29, 93-94, 124
Olivo, Andrew, 144
opposite(s), 13, 32-33, 38, 65, 87, 102,
    108, 126, 129-130
    union of, 97-98, 101, 104-107, 109, 111-
    115, 121-122
opus contra naturam, 88
order, 87
orgasm, 70, 117-119, 121. *See also*
    ejaculate/ejaculation
Otto, Rudolf: *The Idea of the Holy,* 61, 67

pachysandra, 57-59, 61
paradox, 98-100, 125, 131
parent(s)/parenting, 87-88, 135. *See also*
    father/fatherhood; mother/mothering
passion, 123

Studies in Jungian Psychology
by Jungian Analysts

Quality Paperbacks

Prices and payment in $US (except in Canada, $Cdn)

1. The Secret Raven: Conflict and Transformation
Daryl Sharp (Toronto). ISBN 0-919123-00-7. 128 pp. $18

2. The Psychological Meaning of Redemption Motifs in Fairy Tales
Marie-Louise von Franz (Zürich). ISBN 0-919123-01-5. 128 pp. $18

3. On Divination and Synchronicity: The Psychology of Meaningful Chance
Marie-Louise von Franz (Zürich). ISBN 0-919123-02-3. 128 pp. $18

4. The Owl Was a Baker's Daughter: Obesity, Anorexia and the Repressed Feminine Marion Woodman (Toronto). ISBN 0-919123-03-1. 144 pp. $18

5. Alchemy: An Introduction to the Symbolism and the Psychology
Marie-Louise von Franz (Zürich). ISBN 0-919123-04-X. 288 pp. $25

6. Descent to the Goddess: A Way of Initiation for Women
Sylvia Brinton Perera (New York). ISBN 0-919123-05-8. 112 pp. $18

8. Border Crossings: Carlos Castaneda's Path of Knowledge
Donald Lee Williams (Boulder). ISBN 0-919123-07-4. 160 pp. $18

9. Narcissism and Character Transformation: The Psychology of Narcissistic Character Disorders
Nathan Schwartz-Salant (New York). ISBN 0-919123-08-2. 192 pp. $20

11. Alcoholism and Women: The Background and the Psychology
Jan Bauer (Montreal). ISBN 0-919123-10-4. 144 pp. $18

12. Addiction to Perfection: The Still Unravished Bride
Marion Woodman (Toronto). ISBN 0-919123-11-2. 208 pp. $20

13. Jungian Dream Interpretation: A Handbook of Theory and Practice
James A. Hall, M.D. (Dallas). ISBN 0-919123-12-0. 128 pp. $18

14. The Creation of Consciousness: Jung's Myth for Modern Man
Edward F. Edinger (Los Angeles). ISBN 0-919123-13-9. 128 pp. $18

15. The Analytic Encounter: Transference and Human Relationship
Mario Jacoby (Zürich). ISBN 0-919123-14-7. 128 pp. $18

17. The Illness That We Are: A Jungian Critique of Christianity
John P. Dourley (Ottawa). ISBN 0-919123-16-3. 128 pp. $18

19. Cultural Attitudes in Psychological Perspective
Joseph L. Henderson, M.D. (San Francisco). ISBN 0-919123-18-X. 128 pp. $18

21. The Pregnant Virgin: A Process of Psychological Transformation
Marion Woodman (Toronto). ISBN 0-919123-20-1. 208 pp. $20

22. Encounter with the Self: A Jungian Commentary on William Blake's
Illustrations of the Book of Job
Edward F. Edinger (Los Angeles). ISBN 0-919123-21-X. 80 pp. $18

23. The Scapegoat Complex: Toward a Mythology of Shadow and Guilt
Sylvia Brinton Perera (New York). ISBN 0-919123-22-8. 128 pp. $18

24. The Bible and the Psyche: Individuation Symbolism in the Old Testament
Edward F. Edinger (Los Angeles). ISBN 0-919123-23-6. 176 pp. $20

26. The Jungian Experience: Analysis and Individuation
James A. Hall, M.D. (Dallas). ISBN 0-919123-25-2. 176 pp. $20